P. H. (Patrick H.) Casey

Notes on A history of auricular confession

H.C. Lea's account of the power of the keys in the early church

P. H. (Patrick H.) Casey

Notes on A history of auricular confession
H.C. Lea's account of the power of the keys in the early church

ISBN/EAN: 9783741192678

Manufactured in Europe, USA, Canada, Australia, Japa

Cover: Foto ©Lupo / pixelio.de

Manufactured and distributed by brebook publishing software
(www.brebook.com)

P. H. (Patrick H.) Casey

Notes on A history of auricular confession

NOTES

ON A HISTORY

OF

AURICULAR CONFESSION:

H. C. LEA'S ACCOUNT

OF THE

POWER OF THE KEYS

IN THE

EARLY CHURCH.

BY

REV. P. H. CASEY, S. J.,

PROFESSOR OF DOGMATIC THEOLOGY IN WOODSTOCK COLLEGE.

JOHN JOS. McVEY,
PHILADELPHIA.
1899.

THE POWER OF THE KEYS.

In delivering a series of lectures on the Sacrament of Penance during the current year, the writer of the present pamphlet had frequently to answer objections taken from Mr. Lea's History of Auricular Confession and Indulgences.[1] Owing, however, to the limited number of lectures, it was impossssible to reply in detail to one-half the objections supplied by so extensive a work as Mr. Lea's. So it was decided to select one of the most important questions in his three volumes and subject his treatment of it to a minute analysis. This method, it was thought, might disclose the true character of his work, and allay any anxiety that might exist as to the difficulties that were left unanswered. Accordingly, a vital question was selected, the historian's authorities were examined, his arguments were proposed and refuted, many of them needing no more refutation in a class of Theology than merely to be read. It has been thought good, however, to expand the answers then given and illustrate them for popular use, not so much for the sake of replying to Mr. Lea on one particular subject, as to bring into clearer light the character of his work and the constant unfairness of his methods. It is bad enough to find a historian wrong

[1] A History of Auricular Confession and Indulgences in the Latin Church. By Henry Charles Lea, LL.D. Lea Brothers & Co. Philadelphia. 3 vols. 8vo.

here and there on important matters, but to find him
constantly and persistently wrong on the vital question
of his whole investigation is a discovery that renders
further examination useless ; the rest of his work may
be read as a curiosity, but not as a history—not even as
a history that one might think it worth his while to
refute.

Though Mr. Lea is not to be ranked among the his-
torians of Auricular Confession, but among its most
prominent antagonists, still he is not one of those
ignorant declaimers who rail against Confession as if
the very word conjured up some unpleasant memories
of their own misdoings. Mr. Lea is a man of varied
learning, and displays at times a knowledge of Catholic
Theology that is rarely found in a layman outside the
Catholic Church.   He is, moreover, a man of much
reading and of extensive research ; and his three octavo
volumes are a monument, if not to his honesty, at least
to his toil.[1]   In them he has gathered together everything that has been considered as telling against Confession and Indulgences since the time that St. Peter
censured Simon Magus and referred him to God for for-

[1] Short but telling criticisms of Mr. Lea's work considered as a
whole may be found in the *Dublin Review*, (Oct. 1897), in the *Tablet*, (Nov. 21, 1896), and in the *Catholic World*, (March 1897). The
learned reviewers seem to regard Mr. Lea's methods more as the
effect of incompetency than of guile. Dr. Bouquillon in an able
article on Mr. Lea's "Chapters from the Religious History of
Spain, etc," (*Cath. Quarterly*, Jan. 1891,) exercises the same
charitable forbearance. Those who think that Catholic critics are
too severe on Mr. Lea would do well to consult the *Athenæum* of
September 19, 1896.

giveness. The author's array of references at the foot of nearly every page invests his work with an appearance of scholarship that has passed with many as a convincing proof of his reliability. Indeed, his collection of references looks like a direct challenge to his opponents. It is precisely here that we find the chief cause for complaint. For it is principally by means of references and quotations that Mr. Lea has succeeded in some quarters in passing himself off as a historian. His references, besides, are remarkably accurate, considering their multitude; and as far as titles and numbers are concerned, they call for little censure. This of itself has deceived many. But the question is, What have we behind the references, titles and numbers? This is what we are going to investigate. At the end of the pamphlet we shall give a reprint of Mr. Lea's preface and of the pages and references subjected to examination.

Our historian announces in his preface that he is not going "to thresh old straw." He has sought to view the subject from a new stand-point, and to write a history, not a "polemical treatise." Now, in a history of auricular Confession, no one can fail to see the importance attaching to the *History of the Keys during the first five centuries of Christianity*. The Church's power of absolving from post-baptismal sin, or as it is technically called, the Power of the Keys, is the doctrine on which the theory and practice of auricular Confession are based. The fundamental question then in this whole matter when considered from a historical point of view is, Did the Church of the first five centuries be-

lieve that Christ had given to His Apostles and their
successors the power of forgiving sin as now claimed by
the Church of Rome? It is to this important question
that Mr. Lea addresses himself in the seventh chapter
of his first volume. He has little to say, however,
about the power as granted to the Apostles. It is with
the transmission of it that he is specially concerned.
However, as he leaves his rôle of historian and touches
quite misleadingly on the character of the power itself,
we must begin with him on this point.

After quoting the two texts from St. Matthew (xvi.
19; xviii. 18), in which Christ is recorded as giving to
St. Peter and then to the other Apostles the power of
loosing and binding, Mr. Lea gives the classic text
from St. John (xx. 23): "Whose sins you shall forgive, they are forgiven; and whose sins you shall retain, they are retained." On this text, which is the
chief source of proof for the Catholic dogma of the forgiveness of sins, our historian makes the following
comment in a note (p. 107):

"The orthodox explanation of the reiteration of the
grant of power by Christ after His resurrection is that
in Matthew He merely made a promise, the fulfilment
of which is recorded in John."

By this, of course, Mr. Lea means that to find out
the meaning of the text in St. John we must go back
to the texts in St. Matthew. We are glad to find him
admitting that in the power of *loosing* and *binding*,
Christ had promised to His Apostles what He Himself
afterwards called the power of remitting and retaining
sin. That such power is contained in the metaphor

of *loosing* and *binding* might be denied by some. Now, to find out the exact meaning of this power which was first expressed in metaphor, we ought to go to where the same power is conveyed in language which, according to the usage of the New Testament, is never metaphorical. Such is the language of Our Divine Lord to His Apostles in the text : "Whose sins you shall forgive, they are forgiven." Wherever there is mention made in the New Testament of the *remission of sin*, there is always question of the true and real forgiveness of the offence. Now Mr. Lea inverts the ordinary laws of Scriptural interpretation when he tries to bring us back to a metaphorical phrase to show us the meaning of a text that is couched in the plain and literal language of Holy Writ. Instead of this, he might have suggested—for he is quite fond of suggesting such little things—that the Apostles could have hardly understood the words of their Divine Master in any other sense than that in which so often before they had heard Him speak of the "remission of sin." In like manner, instead of telling us what Fr. Palmieri says about the power of *retaining* sin—a question not now under discussion—Mr. Lea might have told us what a non-Catholic writer thinks about the power of remitting sin as spoken of in St. John xx. 23. E. Mellor, D. D., a writer no less hostile to Catholic tenets than is Mr. Lea himself, says on this text :

"I cannot pretend to challenge the doctrine of auricular Confession and priestly absolution on *a priori* grounds, as if it were impossible for God Himself to invest an order of men with such stupendous power. He who can communicate the gift of tongues and

prophecy and healing and miracle, cannot consistently
be regarded as incapable of deputing the ghostly function in question.   And further, I cannot imagine that
on the supposition that such authority was confided to
mortal men, it could have been conveyed in terms
more precise or more appropriate than those now under
consideration.   These concessions I make without reserve as due in all candor to the Confessionalists, whatever consequences they may be supposed to involve."[1]

But laying aside the question of exegesis into which
our historian so quickly lapsed, we shall take up his
statements about the transmission of the Keys.   After
quoting the texts in which the power of "loosing"
and "binding" and "remitting sin" was granted to
St. Peter and the other Apostles by our Divine Lord,
Mr. Lea says (p. 108):

"Whatever sense may be attributed to this grant of
power, the primitive Church *evidently* regarded it as
personal to the holy men whom Christ had selected as
His immediate representatives."

We have italicized the word "evidently."   If it be
evident that the Fathers of the primitive Church considered this power as a personal gift conferred on the
Apostles, Mr. Lea must have some testimony that
evidently proves this.   Let us see what our historian
regards as *evidence*.

"At the time the gospels were composed, the Apostles were not expected to have any successors, for
Christ had foretold the coming of the Day of Judgment
before that generation should pass away,[2] and the pres-

[1] Priesthood in the Light of the New Testament.   Third Ed., p. 325.

[2] Does not Mr. Lea's reasoning make our Divine Lord guilty of a false prediction?

ence of this in all the synoptic gospels shows how universal among Christians was the expectation of its fulfilment." (Lea, p. 108.)

At the time St. John's gospel was composed, and therefore when the text, "Whose sins you shall forgive," etc., was written, the Apostles were not only expected to have successors, but most of them actually had them; for, with the exception of St. John and perhaps St. Philip, they had already gone to their reward and had left successors to carry on their work. St. John wrote his gospel between A. D. 80 and A. D. 95. Now St. Peter and St. Paul were put to death about the year 64; St. James the Less about the year 63, and St. James the Greater about 42. Here at least are four Apostles who had successors, and even for a period varying from twelve to nearly forty years before the gospel of St. John was written. And this is the source from which we take our chief proof for the Church's power to remit sin.

But why should we limit ourselves to the gospel of St. John? According to Harnack's chronology, the gospel of St. Mark was written probably A. D. 65–70; that of St. Matthew probably A. D. 70–75, and St. Luke's A. D. 78–93. If these dates be correct, then St. Peter, St. Paul, St. James the Greater, and St. James the Less had successors in the ministry before any gospel was written.

Again, what does Mr. Lea mean by saying that Christ had foretold the coming of the Day of Judgment before that generation should pass away, and consequently the Apostles were not expected to have any successors?

Christ's prediction, if rightly understood, could not give rise to any such expectation. Nor is there a shadow of proof that the Christians of Apostolic times understood the words of our Divine Lord as implying that the Day of Judgment would come before those who were then living would have passed away. The early Christians may have understood the words, as most orthodox writers do, as applying to the Jewish race or the destruction of Jerusalem. But apart from this, St. John and the members of the Churches for whom he wrote were all "early Christians"—many of them "very early"—and no matter what they thought about the end of the world, they lived long enough to know that the Apostles would have successors in the work of their ministry—they had seen the successors appointed. Furthermore, any belief that the early Christians may have had about the End, did not prevent them from knowing that the Church would last, and so would its ministry, as long as the world lasted. "Behold I am with you all days, even to the consummation of the world." (Matt. xxviii. 20). These words addressed to the Apostles were proof enough that they were to have successors as long as time endured. Finally, Mr. Lea's argument proves no more against the transmission of the Power of the Keys than it does against the transmission of the power of administering Baptism or of consecrating the Eucharist.

SAINT PETER.

But our historian resumes (p. 108):

"In fact how slowly the idea was developed that the Apostles had this power is seen in Philip referring Simon

Magus to God for forgiveness after repentance and in
the legend related above from Eusebius of St. John and
the robber."

It was not Philip who referred Simon Magus to God
for forgiveness, it was St. Peter. (Acts viii. 19). But
letting this pass as a mere slip, is Mr. Lea so simple as
to imagine that if St. Peter had the Power of the Keys
he should have turned to the hypocrite Simon Magus
and said : "Simon, go down on your knees and make
your confession," or "Simon, come to me and I will
absolve you"? What Simon stood in need of was not
advice about Confession or apostolic absolution. What
he needed was the fear of God and prayer for the grace
of repentance. St. Peter addressed him just as any
good, sensible priest of to-day would address a sinner
of the same character. "Thy heart is not right in the
sight of God. Do penance, therefore, for this thy
wickedness ; and pray to God if perhaps this thought
of thy heart may be forgiven thee." (Acts viii. 21-22.)
To score a point in favor of his view, Mr. Lea says
that Simon is referred to God for forgiveness "after"
repentance. Where is this in the text? Because Simon
is told "to do penance and to pray," does it follow
that he must do penance first, and pray afterwards?
In the same manner we should be obliged to obey the
command, "Watch and pray," by first watching and
afterwards praying. I merely call attention to this
point to show our historian's method of reading his
preconceived view into history. A humble prayer for
forgiveness may be one of the very first acts of true
repentance.

SAINT JOHN.

But says Mr Lea (p. 108):

"Had the belief existed, the Apostle John would not have been represented as offering his own soul in exchange and as interceding long and earnestly with God ; as soon as assured of the sinner's repentance he would have been recorded as absolving him."

True, St. John is represented as praying long and earnestly for the robber's conversion. Therefore, he did not have the power of forgiving sin ! If this be so, then it is absurd for a Catholic priest who believes he has such power, to intercede long and earnestly with God for a man's conversion, or to offer up his life, if needs be, for the grace of sorrow for some poor sinner. What nonsense ! Moreover, how does Mr. Lea know that if St. John had the Power of the Keys "he would have been recorded as absolving" the robber? Is the Apostle recorded as giving him the Blessed Eucharist? He is not. Will Mr. Lea therefore oblige us to conclude that there existed at the time no belief in the Sacrament of Christ's Body and Blood? St. Clement, from whom Eusebius (H. E. III. 23) transcribes the story, tells us that after the robber's repentance, St. John spent several days with him until he reconciled him to the Church. There was no need of adding that the Apostle gave him absolution. If this was one of the ordinary conditions of reconciliation, there was no special reason why St. Clement should be found recording its fulfilment.

But continues our historian:

"The early Christians would have stood aghast at

the suggestion that God would confer such awful authority on every vicious and ignorant man who might have succeeded in obtaining ordination." (p. 108.)

The early Christians must have stood aghast at the fact that Christ had conferred on Judas the power of administering Baptism and of working miracles! Mr. Lea told us that he was going "to write a history," and not "to thresh old straw." Now, to use his own phrase, it looks like "threshing old straw," to assert that the power of forgiving sin is conferred on every ignorant and vicious priest who happens to succeed in obtaining ordination. Jurisdiction, at least in all the fulness required for giving absolution, is not conferred on a priest by virtue of the Sacrament. His promotion to Holy Orders places him on the list of lawful candidates for the office of Confessor. But he cannot enter on the office, or discharge any of its judicial functions, till he has received appointment from his ecclesiastical superiors. In this appointment he receives jurisdiction, at least in its complete and operative form. Even though Ordination has placed him on the eligible list, still no jurisdiction is granted him unless he has passed a rigorous examination in everything pertaining to the duties of his office. It is said that Gury, the famous Moral Theologian, failed seven times in trying to pass this examination. After a priest has been appointed Confessor, if he proves himself unworthy of the office, he is deprived of his power and loses all right to absolve from sin. In a word, he is suspended. Possibly, this is not enough for Mr. Lea. Well, let him remember how Christ admitted Judas into His own sacred company, and never deprived him of the powers then conferred upon him. The traitor was tolerated to the end, and his first suspension was by his own hand. Mr. Lea, no doubt, is familiar with a very striking passage on the dignity of the Priesthood by St. John Chrysostom. This holy doctor tells the faithful that no matter what the life of the priest may be, if *their* lives are right, God will bestow His Holy Spirit on them through the priest, as of old He bestowed benediction on Israel through Balaam; for the prophet, though a man of unworthy life, could pronounce only blessings on God's people.[1] So after all, Mr. Lea in proposing the above difficulty is merely writing history. The difficulty is an old one, and he gives it as he finds it. Why does he omit the solution which he also finds? He gives us the following remark instead (p. 109): "The transmission of the power from the Apostles to those who were assumed to be their successors is the most audacious *non sequitur* in history." Mr. Lea has no more right to condemn *non sequiturs* than Sir John Falstaff had to condemn lies. Besides, if he is writing a history he ought to give the facts, and let us take care of the *non sequiturs*.

EARLY FATHERS.

"That the primitive Church knew nothing of this is plainly inferable from the silence of the early Fathers. It is proverbially difficult to prove a negative, and in this case, the only evidence is negative." (Lea, p. 109.)

If Mr. Lea's conclusion is "plainly inferable" from

[1] In Joan. Homil. 86, n. 4, Migne LIX. 472.

the writings of the early Fathers, what becomes of the "proverbial difficulty" that he speaks of? He admits that the evidence is only negative. But he continues:

"They [the early Fathers] could not discuss or oppose a non-existent doctrine and practice, and their only eloquence on the subject must perforce be silence; but as they treated earnestly on the methods of obtaining pardon for sins, their omission of all allusion to any power of remission lodged in priest or Church is perfectly incompatible with the existence of contemporaneous belief in it." (p. 109.)

This argument might have force if among the extant writings of the early Fathers there was one single treatise on "the methods of obtaining pardon for sin." But far from finding a single treatise on the subject, we do not come across in their writings a single chapter purporting to give the methods by which sin can be remitted. Moreover, as every one knows, the extant writings of the early Fathers are extremely few. With the exception of the Pastor of Hermas and the short tract called the Didache, we have nothing more than a dozen letters from the Fathers of the first one hundred and fifty years of Christianity. Negative evidence from such limited sources must be very meagre indeed, and Mr. Lea ought not draw conclusions "plainly inferable," when the "proverbial difficulty" of proof becomes far greater than it usually is. But he resumes his argument (p. 109):

"We have seen already (Chap. I.) that St. Clement of Rome, the Didache, Barnabas, St. Ignatius and the Shepherd of Hermas, while counselling sinners as to reconciliation with God, knew nothing of any authority under God."

The authors here referred to touch only incidentally on reconciliation. But even though they had discussed the question expressly in the twelve letters and the two short treatises they have left us, still Mr. Lea's argument would amount to nothing. Let us look at Wiseman's sermon on the "Delay of Repentance,"[1] and St. Alphonsus Liguori's on the Means necessary for Salvation."[2] Both sermons "counsel sinners as to reconciliation with God." Still in neither discourse is there a single word about any "authority under God." Well, eighteen centuries from now, some historian like Mr. Lea, not being able perhaps to find any of Wiseman's or Liguori's writings, except the two sermons here alluded to, will conclude: "It is 'plainly inferable' from these sermons that Liguori and Wiseman knew nothing about the Power of the Keys. Treating expressly on Repentance and the means of Salvation, they could not have omitted speaking of this power if they knew of its existence." Now, considering the subject of these two sermons, this conclusion of our future historian would be founded on far better evidence than the argument Mr. Lea bases on the silence of the Apostolic Fathers.

St. Irenaeus and St. Dionysius.

"Irenaeus asks how sins can be remitted unless God against whom we have sinned remits them to us, and evidently is ignorant of any intermediary function." (Lea, p. 109.)

[1] Sermons on Moral Subjects. Sermon X.
[2] Sermons for the Sundays of the year. Sermon III.

If St. Irenæus' ignorance "of any intermediary function" is evident from the fact that he asks how sin can be remitted unless God remits it, then every Catholic on the face of the earth must be convicted of the same ignorance. The smallest boy in our Catholic Sunday Schools could tell Mr. Lea that no sin can be remitted unless God remits it.

"St. Dionysius of Corinth orders all returning sinners to be received back kindly and says nothing about absolving them." (Lea, p. 109).

The Parish Priest who would admonish his new Curate to receive kindly every returning penitent would feel justly indignant at his Curate's stupidity on finding out that he was receiving back penitents very kindly, but without giving them absolution. Suppose the new Curate had been brought up in Mr. Lea's School of Logic, he might even go further and reason thus: "The Pastor told me to receive my penitents kindly, but he said nothing about absolving them. The venerable man must know nothing about the Power of the Keys."

St. Polycarp.

"The Epistle of Polycarp to the Philippians is a summary exhortation as to conduct and practice in which if confession and absolution were customary he could not avoid referring to them, but he says nothing about them." (Lea, p. 109.)

The great Encyclical of Leo XIII., on Holiness of Life,[1] is "a summary exhortation as to conduct and

[1] De Vita Sancte Instituenda. December 25, 1888. Tablet, Jan. 12, 1889.

2

practice," and there is not a single word in it about
Confession or Absolution. The Pastoral Letter of the
Archbishops and Bishops of the Third Plenary Council
of Baltimore, 1884, is a like "summary exhortation as
to conduct and practice," addressed to the Catholics of
the United States. There is not a single word in it
about Confession or Absolution. Mr. Lea should read
these two epistles and reconsider the force of his evidence from St. Polycarp. But he continues (p. 110):

"Nor in the paragraph as to the duties of priests is
there any allusion to such functions as to mediation between God and man. As for the priest Valens and his
wife who had misbehaved he only says, 'May God
grant them true repentance.'"

Nor in the paragraph as to the duties of priests is
there any allusion to the functions of *baptizing, administering the Eucharist* or *reading the Bible.* St. Polycarp
is laying down general principles of conduct for priests.
As to what he says about Valens and his wife, it is
nothing more than any bishop would say at the present
time about two such characters.[1]

But, says our historian: "The whole epistle of St.
Polycarp pictures a church of the utmost simplicity, in
which man deals directly with his Creator." (p. 110.)

The object of St. Polycarp's epistle was not to picture
the Church. It was to exhort the Christians of Phil-
ippi to the practice of the great virtues that unite man
with God. Mr. Lea has notions fundamentally wrong
as to what bishops should treat of in their pastoral
letters.

[1] S. Polycarpi Epist. ad Phil. c. 6, 11.

But before proceeding further we may answer an objection that may possibly be urged in favor of Mr. Lea's contention. It may be said that his arguments when taken singly may prove but little, but when taken collectively they may prove a great deal. The negative evidence that he advances ought not to be answered piecemeal. The whole weight of the testimony should be taken, and the collective force of the argument considered and refuted. To this I answer that the principle advanced is quite true when in each negative argument there is some intrinsic force of its own. An argument may not of itself be strong enough to bring conviction, but still there may be something in it that reasonably inclines the mind in one direction. In this case, the arguments when taken collectively give a new value, equal, of course, to the sum of their separate values. But if there be no force whatever in the arguments when taken singly, there can be no force in them when taken collectively. If a man claims that by right of inheritance he owns a certain piece of property bequeathed to his family many years ago, there is no use in trying to disprove his claim from documents that make no mention of this piece of property, unless it can be proved that the documents would *necessarily* contain an account of its transfer, if such a thing had ever taken place. What would the testimony amount to, if the documents in the case were not municipal records, wills or testaments, but a few family letters or a few instructions sent by parents to their children? Now this is precisely the character of Mr. Lea's testimony from the early Fathers.

There is no reason whatever why any of the documents he quotes should bear express testimony to the Power of the Keys. In the first place, as we have seen, the documents that survive from those early days are extremely few. May not the absence of positive testimony be owing to the absence of documents? Again, the documents are of such a nature that the absence of positive testimony from their pages is far easier to explain than its absence from numerous Catholic writings of to-day. We have seen several cases of this. Furthermore, sermons and instructions may be heard in our churches Sunday after Sunday without any express mention of priestly absolution. For those who know the teaching of the Church, the very word *penance* suggests absolution, the word *confession* does the same. Can we not suppose this to be also the case in regard to the early Christians? Do not the words *confession* and *penance* frequently occur in the writings of the early Fathers? St. Clement, for example, says in his second epistle (c. 8): "Let us also while we are in this world, repent with our whole heart of the evil deeds we have done in the flesh, for after we have gone out of the world no further power of confessing and repenting will there belong to us." St. Barnabas writes in his epistle (c. 19): "*Confess your sins;* do not come to prayer with a bad conscience; this is the way of light." And in the Didache of the Twelve Apostles we read (c. 14): "Coming together on the Lord's Day, break bread and give thanks, *confessing your transgressions,* that your sacrifice may be pure." How do we know that words such as these did not mean as much for the early Christians as they do for the Catholics of to-day? To suppose that they did not is to beg the question, and this is what Mr. Lea does. But perhaps he has some stronger arguments in reserve, so we shall let him resume.

"In fact the custom which prevailed as we have seen of not admitting Clerics to penance shows that the whole penitential system had nothing to do with the relation between the sinner and his God." (p. 110).

We cannot see that it shows anything of the kind. Clerics of the higher order, that is, bishops, priests and deacons, were exempt from *solemn* and perhaps from all *public* penance; but they were by no means exempt from the obligation of doing penance *in private*. The council of Neo-Cæsarea, A. D. 314,[1] prescribes the penance that priests must be subjected to for certain sins. The council of Elvira, A. D. 313,[2] lays down the penance for deacons. The testimony of St. Leo the Great is most explicit on the point. In his epistle to Rusticus, the bishop of Narbonne, he says it is not the custom of the Church for deacons and presbyters to receive penance by the imposition of hands, but such persons when they have sinned must do penance in private. (Unde hujusmodi lapsis, ad promerendam misericordiam Dei, privata est expetenda secessio, ubi illis satisfactio, si fuerit digna, sit etiam fructuosa.)[3]

Again, because Clerics were not allowed to kneel at the entrance of the church and ask the prayers of those who passed in, does it follow that the poor penitents

[1] Can. I. Harduin I. p. 281.
[2] Can. LXXVI. Harduin I. p. 258.
[3] Epist. 167, Migne LIV. 1203.

who did kneel there were not going through a system of penance "that had relation to God"? Let us hear what Tertullian says in his treatise on Repentance: (c. 12:) "If you shrink back from *exomologesis*,[1] consider in your heart hell, which *exomologesis* will extinguish for you; and imagine first the magnitude of the penalty, that you may not hesitate about the adoption of the remedy."[2]

This is what Tertullian, while still a Catholic, tells us about *exomologesis* or the external acts of penance; and nevertheless Mr. Lea assures us that "the whole penitential system had nothing to do with the relations between the sinner and his God."

Our historian continues (p. 110):

"The first allusion to any power of pardoning sin occurs early in the third century, when Tertullian protested vigorously on hearing that it was proposed at Rome to remit the sin of fornication and adultery to those who had duly performed penance. Whether this purpose was carried out or not we have no means of knowing positively, but there is every appearance that the project was allowed to drop, as there is no trace in any subsequent document that adultery was treated with greater mildness than homicide or idolatry—indeed, we have seen that in some African Churches those guilty of it were not even received to penitence. Yet that the subject was beginning to attract attention is shown by Tertullian's argument that the grant to Peter was personal; the Apostles had the power of forgiving sins, and this has been transmitted to the Church; if

---

[1] In the ninth chapter of this treatise, Tertullian defines *exomologesis* as the whole external act of penance.

[2] Edinb. Trans. Tert. I. p. 276, Migne I. 1353.

the bishop of Rome claims it, let him show his right by performing miracles like the Apostles."

It seems to me that no man who is seeking for an impartial history of the Power of the Keys can fail to discover in Tertullian's protest a most telling argument against Mr. Lea's position. The treatise *De Pudicitia*, from which Mr. Lea quotes, was written by Tertullian after he had become a Montanist. St. Zephyrinus was bishop of Rome, and what his belief was as to the Power of the Keys is put beyond dispute by the new advocate of Montanism. It is the old story of heresy bringing into light the inner life and belief of the Church—its family secrets, as it were, guarded so long and reverently as things too sacred to be divulged or even put in writing. "I hear," says Tertullian, "there has been an edict set forth, and a peremptory one too. The Sovereign Pontiff—that is, the bishop of bishops, issues an edict: 'I remit to such as have discharged the requirements of penance the sins both of adultery and fornication.' (*De Pudicitia*, c. 1.)[1] 'Exhibit, therefore, even now to me, apostolic sir, prophetic evidences that I may recognize your divine virtue, and vindicate to yourself the power of remitting such sins.' (c. 21.)[2] But you say, 'The Church has the power of forgiving sins.' This I acknowledge and adjudge more than you, I who have the Paraclete Himself in the persons of the new prophets, saying: 'The Church has the power to forgive sins, but I will not do it lest they commit others withal.'"[3]

---

[1] Migne II. 1032. [2] Migne II. 1078.

[3] Edinb. Trans. Tert. III. p. 57, 117, Migne, l. c.

Here is Tertullian the Montanist claiming to be
directed by the Holy Spirit in the persons of Montanus,
Maximilla and Priscilla, and opposing his views to
those of St. Zephyrinus. Which of the two men shall
we accept as a witness to the belief of the Church at
that time?—a man under the influence of Ecstatics, or
St. Zephyrinus, "the bishop of bishops" according to
Tertullian's own phrase, and a man against whom no
word was ever spoken except by the followers of Montanus? In writing eighteen centuries from now the
history of Catholic belief in the nineteenth century, to
whose testimony will the just and upright historian
have recourse?—to that of Leo XIII., or to that of some
learned but misguided ecclesiastic who had fallen under
the influence of a coterie of visionaries! But this is
not all.

Mr. Lea's quotation would lead us to imagine that
St. Zephyrinus was starting an innovation, and that
Tertullian merely protested on behalf of the orthodox
Church. Now it is clear from Tertullian's own testimony that the reverse is the case. Tertullian was the
innovator, and his protest was not only against Zephyrinus but against the Church—against the faith which
even he himself had professed. In the very first chapter of his treatise *De Pudicitia*, after attacking the edict
of St. Zephyrinus, he says: "This too, therefore, shall
be a count in my indictment against the Psychics,[1] as

---

[1] He gives the name of Psychics to the Catholics as indicating
their naturalism. He reserves for himself and his followers the title
of Pneumatici as indicating their guidance by the Holy Ghost.
Migne II. 979.

well as againt the *fellowship of opinion* (*sententiæ soci-etatem*) which I formerly maintained among them, that they may the more cast this in my teeth for a mark of fickleness." [1] He then goes on to say that he need not be ashamed of his fickleness, if it is a profitable one. He does not "blush at ceasing to hold what he has discovered to be an error." So when Tertullian first became a member of the Catholic Church, he found in it the belief which he now repudiates. By "a special revelation of the Paraclete" he discovers that what he had been taught at the time of his Baptism was wrong. He will attack it. He will take from priests and bishops the power of forgiving sins, at least the sins of adultery and fornication. He will take from men and women the power of contracting a second marriage. If a man commits adultery, he must go to God alone for forgiveness; if his wife dies, he must embrace a life of continence. Zephyrinus is wrong; the Church of Rome is wrong, so is the Church in Africa. Tertullian *was* also wrong. But he has discovered his error. He has outgrown the old faith, he has become a Montanist; and as such we freely admit that he is on Mr. Lea's side.

"The idea gradually made its way in some churches, though under varying conditions." (Lea, p. 110.) Of course Mr. Lea means that he finds the idea grad-ually expressed with greater frequency and clearness, as the documents that survive from those early days begin to be more numerous and extensive.

[1] De Pudic., c. 1, Migne II. 1033.

SAINT HIPPOLYTUS.

"Not long after Tertullian the canons of Hippolytus in the ritual of episcopal consecration show that God was prayed to bestow on the bishop the power of remitting sins, and the Apostolical Constitutions based on these canons have nearly the same formula at the close of the third century." (Lea, p. 110.)

Here is certainly a remarkable fact. Mr. Lea is ridiculing the idea of the early Church having made any serious pretence to the power of remitting sin. So far, he has offered us only five pieces of positive testimony on the subject; the testimony of St. Zephyrinus, of St. Hippolytus, of the author of the Apostolical Constitutions, of Tertullian the Catholic, and of Tertullian the Montanist. Of these five witnesses, four are against Mr. Lea; only Tertullian the Montanist is with him.

"How completely dependent on local usage however was this claim is seen in the ordination of priests. In the Canons of Hippolytus the same prayer was used for them as for bishops; in an Egyptian Ordo based on the Canons, the prayer for the priest has no allusion to the remission of sins, and the same is observable in the Apostolic Constitutions." (Lea, p. 111.)

If Mr. Lea had not been so anxious to rebut by one of his negative arguments the strong positive testimony that he sees introduced against him, he might have told us that in the ordination of priests there was no need whatever of mentioning the power of forgiving sin. This power is the power of jurisdiction, which may or may not be given to a priest *at the time* of his ordination. Hence in some rituals it may have been mentioned, in others entirely omitted. So Mr. Lea's rebuttal is rather a confirmation of the Catholic doctrine.

ORIGEN.

"Thus in some Churches the bishops were claiming the Power of the Keys, but in others their pretensions were ridiculed. Origen tells us that they cited the text in Matthew as though they held the power to bind and to loose; this is well if they can perform the works for which Christ made the grant to Peter, but it is absurd in him who is bound in the chains of his own sins to pretend to loosen others, simply because he is called a bishop." (Lea, p. 111.)

I will not accuse Mr. Lea of wilfully misrepresenting Origen. But it is very hard to understand how any man could have read the passage in Origen here referred to, without seeing that this author positively affirms that the power of forgiving sin resides in the Church. He denies that it is possessed by those who are so blinded by their sins as to be incapable of judging justly. But bishops who lead virtuous lives and are a source of edification to their people, possess the power and exercise it. Here are Origen's own words:

"Against him, therefore, who judges unjustly, and binds on earth not according to the word of God, and loosens not according to His judgment, against him the gates of hell prevail. He, however, against whom the gates of hell do not prevail judges justly. Therefore he has the Keys of the Kingdom of heaven, opening to those who are loosed on earth that they may be loosed and freed in heaven, and closing to those who by his just judgment have been bound on earth, that they may be bound and condemned in heaven."[1]

[1] In Matt. Tom. XII. n. 14, Migne XIII. 1013.

Then after stating how bishops claim the Power of the Keys, and assert that what they bind or loose on earth is bound or loosed in heaven, Origen adds: "It must be said that they speak correctly, if they have the deed (ἔργον) on account of which it was said to Peter: 'Thou art Peter'; and if they are such that upon them the Church is builded up by Christ, then that word may be rightly applied to them. But the gates of hell ought not prevail against him who wishes to loose and bind."[1]

That Origen withheld this power from men who lacked the faith of Peter and whose lives did not edify the Church, is not to be wondered at when we consider the character of the man. But that Mr. Lea should try to pass off Origen as a witness against the Power of the Keys is simply amazing. If our historian had any doubt as to Origen's meaning in the foregoing passage, why did he not consult the following passage in the same author and let us too have the benefit of seeing it? In his treatise *De Oratione*, Origen says:

"All of us therefore have power to remit the sins committed against us, as is clear from the words, 'As we forgive them who trespass against us,' and, 'If we also forgive every one that is indebted to us.' But he on whom Jesus hath breathed as He did on His Apostles, and who by his fruits can be known to have received the Holy Ghost, and to have been made spiritual so as to be led by the Spirit of God, as sons are, to do what is reasonably done, he remits what God would remit and retains sins that are incurable; ministering to God who alone has power to remit sin, as the pro-

[1] l.c.

phets ministered to Him in speaking not their own
thoughts but the thoughts that His divine will com-
manded.[1] That this is so, is learned from what is said
in the Gospel of St. John concerning the power of remission granted to the Apostles: 'Whose sins you shall
forgive they are forgiven, and whose sins you shall
retain they are retained.' "

Without any reference to this telling testimony from
Origen, or its beautiful illustration as to how God may
employ men to remit sin as He employs them to fore-
tell the future, Mr. Lea continues:

"Evidently to Origen ordination conferred no such
power, to him the priest was a mediator who propitiated God at the altar." (p. 111.)

So to every good Catholic, the priest is a mediator
who propitates God at the altar. But propitation at
the altar does not exclude propitation in the Confessional. Before giving absolution the priest prays over
the penitent for God's merciful forgiveness. In fact, the
few essential words of absolution are found in the very
middle of a prayer of propitiation.

SAINT CYPRIAN.

" We have already seen that Cyprian disclaimed all
power to absolve; the Church could condemn by refusing reconciliation, but those whom it admitted to peace
were only referred to the judgment of God to confirm or
annul the decision." (Lea, p. 111.)

[1] Ὁ δὲ ἐμπνευσθεὶς ὑπὸ τοῦ Ἰησοῦ, ὡς οἱ ἀπόστολοι, . . . ἀφίησιν ἃ
ἐὰν ἀφῇ ὁ θεός, καὶ κρατεῖ τὰ ἀνίατα τῶν ἁμαρτημάτων· ὑπηρετῶν,
ὥσπερ οἱ προφῆται ἐν τῷ λέγειν οὐ τὰ ἴδια, ἀλλὰ τὰ τοῦ θείου βουλήματος
τῷ θεῷ, οὕτω καὶ αὐτὸς τῷ μόνῳ ἐξουσίαν ἔχοντι ἀφιέναι θεῷ.

De Oratione, n. 28, Migne XI. 528.

Yes, according to Mr. Lea's interpretation of Cyprian
as given in the second chapter of this history. (p. 10.)
But not in one single passage of the three referred to by
Mr. Lea does St. Cyprian disclaim the power of remitting sin. On the contrary, in one of the passages his
claim to the power is rather asserted than denied. In
his epistle to Antonianus he says:

"Moreover we do not prejudge when the Lord is to
be the judge; *save* that if He shall find the repentance
of the sinners full and.sound, He will then ratify what
shall have here been determined by us. If, however,
any one should delude us with the pretence of repentance, God, who is not mocked, and who looks into
man's heart, will judge of those things that we have
imperfectly looked into, and the Lord will amend the
sentence of his servants." [1]

So the power to absolve that St. Cyprian disclaims is
the power to do so when the sinner *feigns* repentance.
The priest passes sentence, but the sentence must be rati-
fied by the Lord. This is exactly what every Catholic
believes. Another passage that Mr. Lea refers to in confirmation of his statement is found in the Saint's letter to
the Clergy, where he says that when no priest is present,
a deacon may grant reconciliation to the lapsed at the
moment of death.[2] From this, our historian argues
that reconciliation to the Church did not involve the
exercise of any priestly power of forgiving sin. (Lea,
p. 10.) This is bad logic. It reasons from the particular to the universal; from the exceptional to the

[1] Edinb. Trans. Cyp. I. p. 143; Epis. 10. al. 51. n. 18, Migne
III. 808.
[2] Epis. 12, Migne IV. 264.

ordinary method of reconciliation. According to an opinion, somewhat common at the time, but now grown obsolete, St. Thomas says,[1] that a dying man, if in sin, ought to confess to a layman if he cannot get a priest to hear his confession. Therefore, St. Thomas held that in the ordinary method of confessing there was no sacramental exercise of the Power of the Keys ! This is precisely the character of Mr. Lea's argument. As to the imposition of hands performed by deacons, it is not hard to understand how by that ceremony a deacon might remove from a dying man the sentence of excommunication, or finding him truly contrite, might transfer to his account the indulgence which the martyrs by their certificates had requested for him. In fact, in the very passage referred to, St. Cyprian is speaking of these certificates.[2] No logic will prove that, because a deacon received a dying penitent back into the communion of the Church without absolving him, a priest would also have received him without absolution. If Mr. Lea would drop logic and keep to history, as he promised, he would save us the pain of dwelling on so many miserable arguments.

"In another passage he [Cyprian] is still more emphatic. Let no one, he says, deceive himself, for none but Christ can pardon; man is not greater than God, nor can the servant condone an offense committed against his master." (Lea, p. 111.)

What St. Cyprian means is clear from the context, and would be clear from the passage translated by Mr.

[1] Supplem. q. 8, a. 2.
[2] Cf. Palmieri de Pœnitentia, p. 166.

Lea, if the translator had not omitted a very important phrase. The Saint is inveighing against the rashness of those priests who with undue haste grant full pardon to the lapsed whenever it is applied for. This might be done if the pardon which the priest grants were *his own* grace and indulgence. But it is not. It is the grace and pardon of God who alone can forgive the sin committed against Him. Here are St. Cyprian's own words:

"Man cannot be greater than God, nor can the servant remit by *his own* indulgence (*nec remittere aut donare indulgentia sua servus potest*) what has been committed by a graver crime against the Lord."[1]

By supplying the phrase *sua indulgentia* which Mr. Lea refused to render into English, we have not only the exact meaning of St. Cyprian, but also the exact teaching of Catholics. The Lord must be besought. His forgiveness must be asked. If He is not willing to forgive, in vain does the priest, his servant, offer pardon. The pardon must come from God, though it may come through the priest. None, but God, can remit sin by his own individual authority. "But if any one," says the Saint, "by an over-hurried haste rashly thinks that he can give remission of sin to all, (*remissionem peccatorum dare se cunctis* putat posse,[2] or dares to rescind the Lord's precepts, not only he does not benefit the lapsed, but he injures them. To act thus is to provoke the Lord's anger, not to obey His will; it is

---

[1] De Lapsis n. 17, Migne IV. 494.

[2] De Lapsis. n. 18, Edit. Vindobonæ, 1868; Migne IV. 495.

to forget that His mercy must *first* be implored; it is to despise the Lord and to presume on *one's own power*, (contempto Domino *de sua* facultate præsumere)." When St. Cyprian declares that "none but Christ can pardon sin," he merely excludes, as the whole context shows, every other self-sufficient and independent power. When we say "none but God can raise the dead," "none but God can reveal the future," we merely reject all other power *independent* of God's. We by no means exclude *ministerial* power such as that exercised by the Apostles and the Prophets. In like manner, when the Fathers say that "God alone can remit sin," they do not exclude the possibility or the fact of God's employing a minister through whom He may exercise that power. If it had been St. Cyprian's intention to deny *all ministerial* power of forgiving sin, he could never have written the following passage: "Whence we perceive that only they who are set over the Church and established in the Gospel law, and in the ordinance of the Lord, are allowed to baptize and to give remission of sins, (remissam peccatorum dare)." [1]

Even Tertullian, after he had become a Montanist, would not base an argument against the Power of the Keys on the fact that "God alone can remit sin." The Novatians sometimes abused the phrase, but Tertullian knew too well its correct meaning. In the twenty-first chapter of his treatise *De Pudicitia* he says:

"And so, if it were agreed that even the blessed Apostles granted any such indulgences to any crime, the pardon of which comes from God, not from man,

[1] Ad Jubaianum. Epist. 73, n. 7, Migne III. 1159.

3

it would be competent for them to have done so, not in the exercise of discipline but of power. For they both raised the dead which God alone can do, and restored the debilitated to their integrity which none but Christ can do; nay, they inflicted plagues too which Christ would not do."[1]

"The most that he [Cyprian] will admit is that the intercession of priest and martyr may incline God to mercy and change the sentence." (Lea, p. 112.) How can Mr. Lea make such an assertion as this with the following words of Cyprian before him on the very opposite page:

"All these warnings being scorned and contemned— before their sin is expiated, before confession has been made of their crime, before their *conscience has been purged* by sacrifice *and the hand of the priest*, before the offence of an angry and threatening God has been appeased, violence is done to His body and blood."[2]

St. Cyprian is speaking of those who approach the Holy Table in the state of mortal sin. He upbraids them for doing so. They must have recourse to the priest to have their conscience cleansed. Why did Mr. Lea omit a passage of so much significance for Catholics? Why does he omit the following passage found in number 29 of the same treatise on the Lapsed:

"I entreat you, beloved brethren, that each one should confess his own sin, while he who has sinned is still in this world, while his confession may be received, while satisfaction and the *remission made by the priests* (remissio facta per sacerdotes), is pleasing to the Lord."[3]

---

[1] Edinb. Trans. Tert. III., p. 117; Migne II. 1077.

[2] Edinb. Trans. Cyp. I., p. 362, n. 16; Migne IV. 493.

[3] Migne IV. 503.

But continues Mr. Lea:

"It is the height of arrogance according to Cyprian for a man to assume that he can do what God did not concede even to the Apostles—to separate the grain from the chaff and the wheat from the tares." (p. 112.)

If Mr. Lea had given his readers the context from which he takes this passage they would see that St. Cyprian is not speaking at all of priests who give absolution, but of the Novatians who refuse to give it; and who by excluding the Lapsed from the Church, separated the tares from the wheat—a power which was not given even to the Apostles. "*Quanta humilitatis et lenitatis oblivio!*" says St. Cyprian. The very phrase *lenitatis oblivio*, which Mr. Lea omits from his paraphrase, might have shown him that the Saint was condemning not those who use the Keys, but those who refuse to use them.[1]

ST. FIRMILIAN.

Our historian resumes (p. 112):

"A phrase of Cyprian's contemporary, St. Firmilian of Cappadocia, has been quoted as asserting the power of the Keys, but it occurs in his furious letter to Pope Stephen on the re-baptism of heretics, and refers only to the remission of sin in Baptism; that Firmilian made no claim for such power is shown by his assembling a council in support of Novatianus."

In proof of his assertion that St. Firmilian assembled a council in support of Novatian, Mr. Lea refers us to

[1] Cyprian. Ad. Antonianum; Epist. 10, al. 55, n. 25; Migne III. 816; Edinb. Trans. S. Cypr. I., p. 148.

Eusebius (H. E. VI. c. 44.) Now, 1. There is not a single
word in this chapter about *Firmilian.* 2. There is not
a single word in it about a council being assembled *in
support* of Novatian. 3. There is a story told in it of an
old man who is dying and who sends for a *priest* that
he may not die without *absolution.* 4. In the preceding
chapter there is an account of a council that assembled
at Rome and *condemned* Novatian. 5. In the forty-
sixth chapter, Dionysius, the archbishop of Alexandria,
tells how he was invited by Firmilian and several other
bishops to meet them at a council in Antioch where
certain persons were trying to establish the system of
Novatian. According to the *Libellus Synodicus* the
Council was held and Novatian was deposed.[1] Possibly
this is the council that Mr. Lea refers to as having been
assembled by St. Firmilian. But our historian has
done an injustice to the Saint not only by making him
support Novatian, but also by making him address "a
furious letter" to the Pope. The letter was not addressed *to the Pope* but to St. Cyprian, and begins with
the words: "Firmilian to Cyprian, his brother in the
Lord, greeting."[2] In a footnote (p. 112), Mr. Lea
censures Binterim for quoting this letter as having been
written *by St. Cyprian,* and in almost the very same
breath Mr. Lea himself mixes things up and tells us
that the letter was written to *the Pope.* Really, Mr.
Lea's history reads at times as if the historian had
grown weary in the midst of his work, and then went
to sleep, and dreamed, and woke up, and wrote his

[1] Harduin V. 1498; Mansi I. 719, Fleury Tom. II. 1. 7. n. 9.
[2] Migne III. 1202. Epist. 75, Ed. Oxon.

dreams. But somehow his dreams always invest Novatian with a halo. They never seem influenced by the words of St. Cyprian: "Novatian is not in the Church, nor can he be reckoned as a bishop, who succeeding to none, sprung from himself." [1] But we must pass to the next witness against the Keys.

COMMODIANUS.

"Commodianus in his instructions to penitents, says nothing of any priestly ministrations; as he had himself endured a course of penance, he had every opportunity of knowing that the sinner dealt directly with God; nor in his remarks to priests and bishops does he make any allusion to their possession of such authority." (Lea, p. 112.)

One might have imagined from this paragraph that Commodianus had written *a book* of instructions for penitents. But his instructions turn out to be nothing more than twelve lines of verse. If Mr. Lea imagines that Commodianus should have said something about "priestly administrations" in a half-dozen of couplets, our historian must have strange notions about versemaking. The "remarks" that Commodianus addresses to priests and bishops are also embodied in twelve verses.[2]

ST. PETER OF ALEXANDRIA.

Mr. Lea continues (p. 112):

"St. Peter of Alexandria, in 305, in his instructions for the reconciliation of those who had lapsed in the persecution of Diocletian, knows nothing of any power

[1] Ad Magnum, Epist. 76; Migne III. 1187.
[2] Instructiones, n. 49, 69. Migne V. 239, 253.

to remit sin; the Church can only pray that Christ may intercede for sinners with the Father."

In the first place, St. Peter of Alexandria does not use the word "only." This important little word is injected into the sentence by Mr. Lea. Secondly, the instructions quoted from, are not *a volume* of instructions for the reconciliation of the lapsed, but a few remarks urging the faithful to pray for those who had fallen in persecution.[1] Negative testimony drawn from such sources is simply frivolous.

Mr. Lea resumes:

"Yet when a claim such as that inferred in the ordination ritual of the Canons of Hippolytus had once been made, it was sure in the plastic condition of doctrine and practice, to develop with the increasing power and pretensions of the Church as it emerged from persecution to domination." (p. 113.)

We can readily admit development in the exercise of this power. Suppose that for some centuries there was no ecclesiastical law of any kind, obliging the faithful to confess their sins to a priest and receive absolution. Then, in case they fell into sin, they were free on any occasion whatever to regain the state of grace without going to the priest for forgiveness, provided they had at least the implied intention of confessing their sins sometime before death. Christ enacted a law obliging the faithful to have their sins remitted by the priest, but He did not say at what time in life, or with what frequency, or on what occasions. All this He left to the Church to determine according to time and circum-

[1] S. Petri Alex. Can. XI. Migne XVIII. 497.

stances. In this we admit as much development as Mr.
Lea can prove with sound historical arguments. But
he proves development in another way. He says (p.
113):

"Appetite grows by what it feeds on, and it would
have required abnegation not often predicable of human
nature for bishops not to grasp at such authority after
it had been advanced and exercised by a few."

If we wished to be personal, we might remark that
Mr. Lea's appetite for conclusions larger than the premises must be growing. Why does he not conclude that
if this power had been usurped by bishops, "it would
have required abnegation not often predicable of human
nature" for subjects to submit? Or again, if bishops
usurped such authority, why did they allow it to be exercised over themselves? Why did they not exempt
themselves from the obligation of going down on their
knees and confessing their most secret sins to some poor
priest, their own inferior? If bishops submitted to this
legislation of their own accord, they must have had far
more abnegation than Mr. Lea gives them credit for.
Humiliation such as this is not a thing that poor human
nature "grasps at." Nor on the other hand, is sitting
in the Confessional for five or six hours on a Saturday
afternoon, or on the eve of some great feast, a thing "to
grow fat on." It is one of the greatest hardships of the
priesthood. But we let these things pass. We do not
put them forward as arguments for the divine institution of the Keys. We merely hint at them as trifles
for Mr. Lea to ponder on, and we pass to the examination of his next witness.

ACESIUS AT NICÆA.

He says (p. 113):

"There is a hint of this [how bishops grasped at the power of the Keys] in the remark of the Novatian bishop Acesius who attended the Council of Nicæa and subscribed to its canons, but refused to join in Communion with his fellow members, and when asked by Constantine the reason replied that he considered those unworthy of Communion who would admit to the Sacraments a man who had sinned since baptism," etc.

In this passage Mr. Lea has unconsciously furnished us with an argument that will weigh more with any honest man than a thousand proofs such as those that our historian has been putting forward in favor of his view. I shall give the passage, not in Mr. Lea's words but in those of Sozomen himself:

"Since then, says the Emperor, you are of the same opinion [on these decrees], why do you separate yourself from communion? And when Acesius assigned the discussion that had taken place between Novatus and Cornelius in the reign of Decius, and said that he judged unworthy of the Sacraments those who had fallen after Baptism into that sin which the Scriptures call 'the sin unto death,' and that *the remission depended on the power of God alone, not on that of the priests,* the emperor replied: 'Acesius, erect a ladder and mount to heaven by yourself.'"[1]

Here is the testimony of a Novatian bishop as to the faith of the Fathers of Nicæa, A. D. 325. So after all, the Catholics of to-day are holding the very same doctrine as the Fathers of the First Ecumenical Council. Mr. Lea is still defending the opinion of the Novatians,

[1] Sozomen, H. E. I. 22. Migne LXVII. 925.

and like Acesius must erect a ladder and mount to heaven by himself.

LACTANTIUS.

"Still the development of the power of the Keys was wonderfully slow. As Lactantius was not a priest but a philosopher, his testimony on such a subject does not count for much, but *he knows nothing* of the priest as an intermediary; the sinner deals directly with God." (Lea, p. 113.)

I have called attention to the phrase "knows nothing." Mr. Lea constantly uses it as synonomous with the phrase, "says nothing." They are convenient equivalents for his purpose. It is only in the sense of "says nothing" that he informs us of the fact that Lactantius "knows nothing" of the priest as a mediator. "That the sinner deals directly with God," neither Lactantius nor any other good Christian ever denied. This direct intercourse with God is especially had when the sinner repents of his sin; and it is precisely of this repentance that Lactantius is speaking in the three passages referred to by Mr. Lea.[1]

SAINT HILARY.

"St. Hilary of Poitiers is a more significant witness, and in his commentary on Matthew he seems ignorant of the claim that the power of binding and loosing was conferred on the Apostles to be transmitted to their successors. He treats it wholly as a personal grant to them and makes no allusion to any other view of the matter." (Lea, p. 113.)

[1] Divin. Institt. Lib. IV. c. 17; Lib. VI. c. 13, 24, Edin. Ed. Vol. L p. 254, 388, 415; Migne VI. 501, 684, 722.

On the text of Matthew (xviii. 18), where this power is conferred on the Apostles, St. Hilary has a commentary of only seven lines. The Saint ought not to be blamed for omitting in so brief a passage express mention of a fact which he knew would be taken for granted by those who believed in an *Apostolic* Church. He speaks of the "sentence of Apostolic severity" by which men were to be restrained. He took for granted that as long as the Apostolic Church lasts there will be need of "a sentence of Apostolic severity." Men need restraining now as much as they did in the days of the Apostles, and the sentence that restrains them is no less "Apostolic" than the ministry by which it is exercised.[1]

In a note to the testimony from St. Hilary, Mr. Lea says : "Juenin admits that Hilary does not claim the power as transmitted to the successors of the Apostles, but Palmieri boldly quotes what he says as to the apostolic power, as though he conceded the transmission." (p. 113). Juenin does not admit any such thing as Mr. Lea attributes to him. On the contrary, he quotes the words of St. Hilary to prove the practice of auricular Confession in the fourth century. But it is evident that he could not quote the words for such a purpose unless he considered the Saint as speaking of a power that had been transmitted from the Apostles. To admit that St. Hilary was speaking merely of a power conferred on the Apostles, and then to quote his words as proof of the practice of sacramental Confession in the fourth century, is a contradiction so flagrant,

[1] Hilarius. Commen. in Matth. XVIII. n. 8, Migne IX. 1021.

that it is hard to realize how any writer could have
been so careless as to fix it on Juenin.[1] As for Fr.
Palmieri, when he "boldly quotes" a passage, the
reader should sit down and think before calling the
quotation in question.[2]

SAINT EPIPHANIUS.

"Various other writers of the second half of the
fourth century ascribe no pardoning power to the
Church; the fate of the sinner depends exclusively on
God." (Lea, p. 113.)

For this assertion our historian gives references to
Philastrius, Marius Victorinus and St. Epiphanius.
Now, in the passages referred to, not one of these
writers asserts that the fate of the sinner depends *exclusively* on God. Mr. Lea is constantly giving us his
own epitomized version of the Fathers; and their opinions while passing through his mind are not only modified, but completely altered by such additions as
"only" and "exclusively."[3]

---

[1] Juen. De Poenit. Diss. VI. q. 5, C. I. a. 2, § 3.

[2] In another note on the passage from St. Hilary, Mr. Lea remarks (p. 113): "Possibly his [Hilary's] assertion that the
Pharisees claimed to hold the Keys of the kingdom of heaven (C.
XII. n. 3) may have been intended as a covert rebuke to the high
sacerdotalists."

Is Mr. Lea writing a history of the Keys, or a treatise on the
"possibles"? In the passage referred to from St. Hilary, the rebuke is so "covert," that even our historian who is so eager to find
it can discover nothing more than its bare possibility.

[3] Philastrius Lib. de Haeres, n. 34, Migne XII. 1150; Marius
Vic. Epist ad Ephes. Lib. I. n. 7 (C. I. vers. 7), Migne VIII. 1243;
S. Epiphan. Haeres. 59, Migne XLI. 1018.

Is it not a remarkable fact that St. Epiphanius in his erudite and exhaustive work on heresies, wherein he enumerates all the errors in faith known from the days of the Apostles up to his own times, makes no mention of the power of priests and bishops to remit sin? This is something that should make Mr. Lea pause. If the transmission of the Power of the Keys was an error in faith, why does St. Epiphanius not record it? If some of the early Fathers had written a treatise *ex professo* on the methods of obtaining pardon for sin, and had enumerated, we shall not say 80, (the number of heresies classified by St. Epiphanius), but a dozen or so of such methods, and omitted to say anything about the Power of the Keys, what an invincible argument for his side of the question Mr. Lea would find in the omission! But we must pass to St. Pacian, a contemporary of St. Epiphanius, and see how the so-called error that our historian has been discovering was the teaching of the orthodox Church.

SAINT PACIAN.

"St. Pacianus when controverting the Novatians asserts that the power of the Keys was transmitted to the successors of the Apostles, to be exercised with the utmost caution and only in accordance with the Divine Will; but this was a mere speculative argument, for in his exhortation to sinners he only ascribes to the Church a power to assist, and it is Christ who obtains pardon for us." (Lea, p. 114.)

St. Pacian is an important witness in the case. He was Bishop of Barcelona, a contemporary of Basil, Gregory and Ambrose, and according to St. Jerome,[1]

[1] De Vir. Illust. c. 106; Migne XXIII. 742.

was a man distinguished no less by his virtues than by his words. Of his writings there are extant a discourse on Baptism, an exhortation to repentance, and three letters on the Novatian heresy. Now, in these letters he lays down, as clearly as any Catholic theologian could do, the doctrine of the Keys. His words are so clear that nothing but mere folly would try to explain them away. Mr. Lea admits as much. How then does our historian get over the difficulty? He rushes off to the Saint's exhortation on repentance, and finding in it no express statement about the Power of the Keys, he comes back to the letters written against the Novatians where the power is *expressly* stated and proved. "Ah!" he says, "this is only a speculation! St. Pacian is disputing against adversaries who deny this power; he asserts its existence in the Church; he proves his assertions from Scripture, answers the objections of his adversaries; but he is only speculating." If in these letters on the Novatian heresy, St. Pacian had said nothing about the Power of the Keys, what a telling argument Mr. Lea would have found in the omission. And now when the Saint most explicitly asserts the doctrine, Mr. Lea brushes the assertion aside as "a speculation." A historian takes up Wiseman's sermon on the "Delay of Repentance," and discovers nothing in it about the Power of the Keys. He then turns to the Cardinal's lecture on the Sacrament of Penance, and finding that in it the Power of the Keys is explicitly laid down, proved and defended, he says: "Ah! it is only a speculation; why didn't Wiseman say something about this in his sermon!" But to re-

turn to St. Pacian. Let us see a few of the statements
which our historian refuses to quote and sets aside as
mere speculation. In his third epistle the Saint writes:

"The whole treatise of the Novatians which you have
addressed to me thronged with propositions on all sides,
amounts to this, brother Sympronian: That there is no
room for repentance after Baptism, that the Church cannot *remit mortal sin;* that by the receiving of sinners
she herself perishes. Illustrious honor! Singular authority! Great constancy! To reject the guilty; to
flee the touch of sinners; to have so little confidence in
her own innocence! Who is the assertor of this doctrine, brother? Moses, or Paul, or Christ? . . . None
of these you will say. Who then, I ask? . . . Novatian, you will say, discerned this, but Christ taught it.
Was there then no one of discernment from the advent
of Christ even to the reign of Decius?"[1]

And again:

"'But,' thou wilt say, 'you forgive sin to the penitent, whereas it is allowed to you to remit sin only in
Baptism.' Not to me at all, but to God only, who
both in Baptism forgiveth the guilt incurred, and re-
jecteth not the tears of the penitent. But what I do, I
do not by my own right, but *by the Lord's* . . . . . Where-
fore, whether we baptize, whether we constrain to penance, or *grant pardon to the penitent,* we do this by the
authority of Christ.'"[2]

And lastly says St. Pacian:

"Never would God threaten the impenitent, unless
he would pardon the penitent. 'This,' you will say,
'God alone can do.' It is true. But that also *which
He does through His Priest,* is His own authority. Else

---

[1] Oxford Version, p. 336, 337; Epist. III. n. 1; Migne XIII.
1063.

[2] Oxford Version, p. 343; Epist. III. n. 7; Migne XIII. 1068.

what is that which He saith to the Apostles, 'Whatsoever ye shall bind on earth, shall be bound in heaven, and whatsoever ye shall loose on earth shall be loosed in heaven?' Why said He this, if it was not lawful for men to bind and loose? Is this allowed to Apostles only? Then to them also only is it allowed to baptize, and to them only to give the Holy Spirit, and to them only to cleanse the sins of the nations; for all this was enjoined on none others but Apostles . . . If therefore, the power of the Laver, and of the Anointing, gifts far greater, descended thence to Bishops, then the binding and loosing was with them. Which, although for our sins it be presumptuous in us to claim, yet God who hath granted unto Bishops the name even of His only Beloved, will not deny it unto them, as if holy and sitting in the chair of the Apostles."[1]

In these and in many other passages that we might quote from St. Pacian, we have the doctrine of the Keys stated, proved and defended in the clearest and most positive terms. It is not St. Pacian who is "speculating," it is Mr. Lea.

THE MANICHÆANS.

But continues our historian (p. 114): "The Manichæans seem to have been the first to discover the power of the Keys."

Is not this a slip on Mr. Lea's part? He told us some time ago that Zephyrinus had claimed this power, and that Tertullian had protested against the usurpation. Now Zephyrinus was in his grave before the Manichæan heresy was heard of. The Pontiff died in the year 218, and the founder of the new heresy was

[1] Oxford Version, p. 325, 326; Epist. I. n. 6; Migne XIII. 1057.

only about two years old at the time. According to the
most reliable dates, Manes first appeared in public as a
teacher of the new doctrine about the year 241. Mr.
Lea in hunting up testimony for his view seems to lose
all idea of space and time. But he ought not contradict himself, at least in the same chapter. As to the
Manichæans, every student of history knows that they
borrowed, and modified to suit themselves, the Christian sacraments of Baptism and the Eucharist. If they
claimed the power of forgiving sin and had a sort of
sacrament of Penance, this tells rather in our favor than
against us. They took this third sacrament from where
they took their Baptism and their Eucharist. We are
grateful to our historian for this new argument. But
he resumes (p. 114):

"Their elect could not handle money and when in
want of food would undertake to remit sins for bread.
Ephraim Syrus denounces them bitterly for this; there
is but One who can remit sins, except in the rite of
Baptism."

St. Ephraem is quite right in denouncing the Manichæans; but where does he say that "there is only
One who can remit sin except in Baptism"? Why
does Mr. Lea omit the reference? Instead of telling us
where St. Ephraem makes such an important statement,
he gives us a reference to the almost unknown Protestant writer Wegnern, although he tells us in his preface
that he has abstained from consulting "Protestant
writers," and has "confined himself exclusively to the
original sources and to Catholic authorities."

It was thought good however to supply for Mr. Lea's

omission and have the writings of St. Ephraem searched for the passage quoted by Wegnern. The desired citation was found in the second volume (p. 440) of the Saint's works as published with the Syriac and Latin texts, and it occurs in one of his Hymns against Heresies.[1] The passage quoted in Latin by Mr. Lea in his note (p. 114) is taken from the second strophe of the Hymn, and in it the Saint says nothing more than that the "dogs of Manes," for the sake of their daily bread, wag their tails to everybody they meet, and undertake to remit sin when they stand in need of a crust of bread. "For this they are to be crushed, because there is One alone who can remit sin." Now, in this passage St. Ephraem is evidently speaking of the *principal* and independent cause of forgiveness. For in the very next strophe he expressly states that Christ gave His disciples power to forgive sin. Nor does he say that the exercise of this power is limited to the rite of Baptism. Here are his exact words: "They [the Manichæans] distort according to their caprice the word of the True One who granted to His disciples the power to remit sin only once by water and gave them also the power to loose and to bind." Mr. Lea in giving us the teaching of St. Ephraem combines two strophes into one; he omits the obvious explanation of the first, and perverts the meaning of the other so that St. Ephraem is made to say that "sin can be remitted *only* in Baptism,"

---

[1] Ephraemi Syri opera. Graece et Latine, Tom. 1, 2, 3. Romae 1732, 1746; Syriace et Latine, Tom. 1, 2, 3. Romae 1737, 1740, 1745.

4

whereas what the Saint really says is that "sin can be remitted only *once* in Baptism." There is as much difference between these two statements as there is between the assertions: "It is decreed that we shall die but once;" and, "It is decreed that we shall do nothing but die." Moreover, far from rejecting the Power of the Keys, St. Ephraem asserts it in this very passage. All that he insists on is, that for sin there is no remedy except through penance. Baptism can not be repeated, and the Keys can have no effect without contrition in the sinner. "He whose sins have been bound," he writes, "must pray to Him who remits all sin, so that the All-Redeeming One may through our sorrow sanctify us." And again : "If the All-Sanctifying One makes us just only through sorrow, then it is a swindle for these Bardesanites to undertake, for a bit of bread, to sanctify a man without contrition." (l. c.) Speaking of this very Hymn, J. S. Assemani, the accomplished Syrian scholar, says: "It [the Hymn] speaks very clearly of the Power of the Keys granted to the Church, and lays down the necessity of a laborious penance." "De potestate Clavium Ecclesiæ tradita praeclare loquitur, et laboriosæ Poenitentiæ necessitatem adstruit." [1] So it turns out that St. Ephraem while condemning the Manichæans for usurping the Power of the Keys, also condemns Mr. Lea for rejecting it. It is really interesting to find our historian constantly referring us to passages that refute the very assertion he is trying to prove.

[1] Bibliotheca Orientalis, Tom. i., p. 120.

-◄

SAINT BASIL.

"Possibly this example may have begun to infect
the Church, for his [Ephraem's] contemporary, Basil
the Great, claims that authority to bind and to loose is
lodged with the bishops." (Lea, p. 114.)

Somehow or other Mr. Lea seems to find this heresy
of the Keys always *beginning*. He comes down the
centuries, and wherever he finds any one claiming the
power to absolve from sin, he represents the claim as
something just making its appearance in the Church.
After chasing his prey from its covert, he quite frequently loses the trail, but every time that he discovers
it anew, he says: "Ah! it was here that the thing
started." He told us in the beginning how Zephyrinus
had claimed the Power of the Keys, A. D. 216. He
pointed out how Origen protested against the bishops
who were usurping it, A. D. 245. Now he puts down
St. Basil's claim A. D. 370—a hundred years later—as
a proof that this pernicious doctrine had possibly begun
to infect the Church. We are glad, however, to find
St. Basil admitted as a witness on our side. Has Mr.
Lea anything to offset the testimony of so great a man?
Yes. Basil the Great must have been infected with the
Manichæan heresy. This is not history, it is folly!

"It is highly probable in fact that the Novatian
schism stimulated greatly the progress of Sacerdotalism,
against which it was a protest." (Lea, p. 114.)

Yes, the Novatian heresy brought into clearer light
the teaching of the Church as to the power of remitting
sin, just as the Arian heresy brought out more clearly
the Church's belief in the Divinity of Christ, and the

Manichæan heresy disclosed her teaching as to the
sanctity of marriage.   Mr. Lea continues (p. 114):

"The Schismatics doubtless did not forego the advantage offered them by the hazy and dubious character
of the *pax ecclesiæ* which the priests conferred, and contemptuously asked what was after all the advantage of
the reconciliation purchased at so heavy a cost, and the
orthodox in answering them would naturally be led to
exalt the efficacy of its redeeming power and to assert
that it was equivalent to divine pardon."

We are not surprised to find that those who had
denied the faith and were obliged to submit to a long
term of rigorous penance before being admitted again
into active communion with the Church, should be in-
clined to deny the Power of the Keys.   But that orthodox writers were led thereby to exaggerate the power
into something *essentially different* from what it had been
before, is one of Mr. Lea's "historical possibilities," I
should rather say, "fictions."   It is well known to all
readers of Church history that when the defenders of
orthodoxy went so far as to fall into error themselves,
they shared the fate of those against whom they had
written.   Their defense was repudiated and condemned
as alien to the teaching of the Church.   Thus fared
Eutyches the strenuous opposer of Nestorianism.   Thus
also fared that little band of good and zealous men who
in defending the prerogatives of the Church rejected the
validity of Sacraments conferred by heretics.   Their
opinion may have been very flattering to Church
authorities, but those very authorities denounced it as
foreign to the teaching of Christ.   As to Mr. Lea's
statement about "the hazy and dubious character of

the *pax ecclesiæ*," haze and doubt seem to be no obstacle to his vision. Without thinking that he saw into the very heart of the mist, he never could have assured us, as he has done in Chap. IV. (p. 50), that the imposition of hands was the very *essence* of the ceremony of reconciliation. Less clearness of vision was required to see that this imposition of hands was not "considered as conferring the Holy Ghost." Touching this point, however, our historian has a few remarks that are well worth giving. He writes:

"Yet in some quarters it [the imposition of hands] was held to confer the Holy Ghost, and that this was essential to the redintegration of the penitent in the Church. Thus the Apostolic Constitutions compare it to baptism and represent the Apostles as saying that by it they gave the Holy Ghost to believers. Const. Apost. II. 45. 'Et erit ei in locum lavacri impositio manuum. Nam per impositionem manuum nostrarum credentibus Spiritus Sanctus dabatur." Had this belief been accepted and current this last assertion would have been superfluous. It is perhaps significant that there is nothing of all this in the Canons of Hippolytus." (p. 50, text and note).

Now, here is a fair specimen of Mr. Lea's history— or logic—it is hard to say which. Let me put it into the following shape: "A certain writer, such as Hippolytus, says nothing about the Holy Ghost being conferred by the imposition of hands." "Therefore," says Mr. Lea, "he knew nothing about any such effect." "Very well," we answer, "this is a rather wide conclusion. It is purely negative evidence. But, Mr. Lea, we will quote you an author who *positively* asserts that the Holy Ghost was conferred by the im-

position of hands." "Ah!" says Mr. Lea, "if your
author makes special mention of such a thing, then the
belief in it was not current, for if the belief had been
current, it would have been superfluous to mention it."

Quo teneam vultus mutantem Protea nodo?

If we quote a Father in our favor we are condemned;
if we cannot quote him, we also fall under the ban.
Mr. Lea is urging against us with a vengeance the Cal-
vinistic law:

> "You can and you can't,
> You will and you won't,
> You'll be damned if you do,
> You'll be damned if you don't."

I am not discussing the efficacy or meaning of the
"imposition of hands," or rather I should say of the
various "impositions of hands" that took place in the
process of a sinner's reconciliation to the Church. I
have merely touched on the question to bring out the
character of Mr. Lea's arguments. We must let our
historian proceed.

SAINT AMBROSE.

"This process of exalting the efficacy of reconciliation is well illustrated by the contradictory utterances
of St. Ambrose. Stimulated by conflict with the Novatians, in some passages he asserts the power of the
Keys in the hands of bishops in an unqualified manner;
Christ, he says, could remove sin by a word, but he has
ordered that it should be done through men. Thus he
pushes this to an extent so insane that he represents
God as wishing to be asked to pardon and as virtually
unable to do so without the action of the priests."
(Lea, p. 115.)

If God has enacted a decree that, in case we do not make an act of perfect contrition for our sins, our salvation must depend on priestly absolution; then, by reason of His unchangeable decree, He cannot grant us pardon for sin unless we have recourse to the priest or elicit an act of perfect contrition. Any inability on the part of God in this matter is due to His own immutable decree. Again, according to Catholic teaching, a sinner can at any time have recourse to God and obtain forgiveness by an act of perfect contrition or of perfect love. This act justifies, but not independently of the implicit desire it contains of future recourse to the Keys. This relation to the Keys is the condition under which Almighty God receives it in the present economy as the meritorious cause of justification. We are glad to be informed that a doctrine so completely according to the council of Trent, is defended by St. Ambrose. It is also pleasing to find our historian admitting that St. Ambrose asserts the Power of the Keys. In fact the teaching of the Saint on this point is so clear that there was but one way for Mr. Lea out of the difficulty. He tells us that the Saint made these assertions while "stimulated by conflict with the Novatians." From this explanation one might conclude that St. Ambrose was in a hot oral conflict with the heretics when he uttered the words that tell so strongly against Mr. Lea. The fact is, that every passage but one referred to on this point by our historian was written down calmly and deliberately by St. Ambrose for the instruction of the faithful. The only one that may be looked upon as an exception is taken from the Saint's treatise on

Penance. (Lib. I. c. 7, 8.) But Mr. Lea in the very
next paragraph of his history quotes a passage in his
own favor from this treatise, and puts it down as one
of the passages that St. Ambrose wrote "in his cooler
moments." This is really amusing. A great Doctor
of the Church writes a sentence in which the Catholic
doctrine is clearly expressed. "Oh!" says Mr. Lea,
"he is under the stimulation of conflict." The same
holy Doctor without laying the pen out of his hand
writes down something that seems to favor Mr. Lea.
"Ah! The Saint has regained his self-control! He is
now writing in one of his cooler moments!"

"In cooler moments," says Mr. Lea, "he assumes
that this power is lodged in the Church at large, and
limits it to intercessory prayer, denying that the priest
can exercise any power." (p. 115.)

For the proof of this assertion our historian refers us
to five passages in the writings of the Saint. Now, in
not a single one of these passages does St. Ambrose deny
either explicitly or implicity that the priest has the
power of forgiving sin, nor in a single one of them does
he limit the power of the priest to intercessory prayer.
On the contrary, in the very first passage referred to by
Mr. Lea, instead of a proof of his assertion we have a
most explicit refutation of it. This is the passage:

"They [the Novatians] say that they show reverence
to the Lord for whom alone they reserve the power of
forgiving sins. But none do Him greater injury than
they who rescind his commands and resign *the office*
entrusted to them. For since the Lord Jesus Himself
says in the Gospel, 'Whose sins you shall forgive they
are forgiven, and whose sins you shall retain they are

retained,' who is it that gives Him honor, he who obeys
the command or he who resists?. . . . Both [the power
of loosing and the power of binding] are granted to the
Church, both are not granted to heresy. *For this right
is granted to priests alone* (*jus enim hoc solis permissum sac-
erdotibus est*). Rightly then does the Church that has
real priests (*quæ veros sacerdotes habet*), claim this power,
heresy that has not priests of God cannot claim it. By
not claiming it, heresy passes sentence on itself, that as
not having priests, it must not claim the priestly right,
(*jus sacerdotale*)." [1]

This is the *first* passage to which our historian refers
us for proof of his assertion that St. Ambrose denies
that the priest has any power of forgiving sin! As to
the next *four* passages that Mr. Lea refers to, we find on
consulting Migne that there is not a single line in them
to support his assertion. St. Ambrose is merely urging
the necessity of prayer when there is question of the
conversion of great sinners.[2] The last reference to St.
Ambrose that our historian gives is the treatise *De Spiritu Sancto*, Lib. III. c. 18, n. 137.[3] Here is a literal
translation of the passage:

"Now let us see whether the Holy Ghost condones
sins. But there can be no doubt on this point since the
Lord Himself has said, 'Receive ye the Holy Ghost,
whose sins you shall forgive, they are forgiven.' Behold
how sins are forgiven by the Holy Ghost. *Men give
the use of their ministry for the remission of sin,* (homines

[1] De Poenitentia, Lib. I. c. 2; Migne XVI, 487.
[2] In Luc. Lib., V. Sermo X. n. 11, Migne XV. 1723—In Luc.
Lib. V. Sermo X., n. 92, Migne XV. Col. 1746—In Luc. Lib. VII.
n. 225, Migne XV. 1850.—Ps. 38, Enar. n. 10, Migne XIV. 1093.
[3] Migne XVI. 842.

autem in remissionem peccatorum ministerium exhib-
ent), they do not exercise the right of any power. *For
not in their own name, but in the name of the Father, of the
Son, and of the Holy Ghost do they remit sins,* (neque enim
in suo, sed in Patris, Filii et Spiritus Sancti nomine
dimittunt peccata). They supplicate, the Divinity condones. The service is human, the munificence is of
celestial power."

In this passage, far from denying the priest's power
to forgive sin, St. Ambrose positively asserts it. What
he denies is the priest's *independent* right or power to
condone sin, *for* the priest cannot "act in his own
name;" he must act in the name of the Holy Ghost,
and as His minister. The Divinity condones the
offence through the prayer of absolution. In the time
of St. Ambrose the absolution, as a general rule, was in
the form of a prayer, as it is even to this day in the
Eastern Churches. That the formula was not a mere
intercessory prayer, but a *ministerial act* whereby sin was
remitted is clear from the fact that the power of remitting sin was granted to priests alone. St. Ambrose, as
we have seen, asserts in the clearest terms their exclu-
sive right to this power. But the power of intercessory
prayer was granted to all mankind, to none more fully
than to those who lead holy lives, be they priests or
laymen.

Mr. Lea continues (p. 115):

"And when he [St. Ambrose] came to the practical
exertion of the power he denies that he possesses it and
attributes it solely to God."

As his proof for this assertion our historian gives us
the words of St. Ambrose in the Latin text. This is a

thing he does not do except when the text is extremely strong. So let us examine a specimen of his renditions. The passage occurs in the Saint's well-known letter to the Emperor Theodosius urging him to repentance for the massacre he had been guilty of in Thessalonica.

"Peccatum non tollitur nisi lacrymis et poenitentia. Nec angelus potest, nec archangelus ; Dominus ipse, qui solus potest dicere: ' Ego vobiscum sum,' si peccaverimus, nisi poenitentiam deferentibus non relaxat." "Sin is not taken away except by tears and penance. Neither an angel nor an archangel [can take it away]; the Lord Himself who alone can say, ' I am with you,' (Matt. xxviii. 20), does not forgive, if we sin, unless we repent."[1]

This passage is perverted by Mr. Lea into the three following propositions. 1. St. Ambrose has come to the practical exercise of the power. 2. He denies that he possesses such a power. 3. He attributes it *solely* to God. To this we reply: 1. The king has not yet repented, consequently the Saint has not yet come to the practical exercise of the power. 2. He does not deny that he possesses the power. What he denies is that Angels and Archangels possess it. The Saint was neither one nor the other. He was a man, and the power was given only to men. 3. He does not say that the power belongs *solely* to God. What he asserts is the absolute necessity of penance even when God pardons sin. The Lord who alone could send forth Apostles and promise to be with them in the work of their min-

[1] Ep. 51. n. 11. Migne XVI. 1212.

istry to the consummation of the world, even He does not remit sin except to the penitent.[1]

As to Mr. Lea's perversion of this passage of St. Ambrose, all that I have to say is, if he takes such liberties with a passage the Latin of which he gives us at the foot of the page, what may be the liberties he takes with texts that are buried away in dusty old tomes that only few have the opportunity of consulting?

He concludes his argument from St. Ambrose in these words (p. 115): "His biographer Paulinus tells us that he regarded himself *merely* as an intercessor." (Paulini Vit. S. Ambros. c. 39).[2]

I have italicized the word "merely." It is not found in St. Paulinus; it is one of Mr. Lea's interpolations.

SAINT CHRYSOSTOM.

From St. Ambrose Mr. Lea passes to St. Chrysostom. He accused the great Doctor of the Latin Church of contradictory utterances; he has the same charge to make against the great Doctor of the Greek Church. He writes (p. 115):

"The same inconsistency is found in Chrysostom. We have seen how he assumes that pardon is to be had by almsgiving and other good works. Elsewhere he emphatically declares that no intercessor is needed; God freely forgives those who seek him with heartfelt tears: the prayer of the wicked is much more efficacious with God than any intercessory prayer can be."

[1] According to Catholic teaching, the absolution that the priest gives in the Sacrament of Penance is null and void unless the sinner is sincerely sorry for his sins and has the firm purpose of sinning no more.

[2] Migne XIV. 43.

The teaching of St. Chrysostom which is "inconsistent" with belief in the Power of the Keys, is summed up by Mr. Lea in four propositions. 1. Almsgiving and other good works are very efficacious means of obtaining forgiveness of sin. 2. Without any intercessor, a sinner may go to God and obtain forgiveness. 3. The gravest sin can be blotted out by perfect contrition. 4. A sincere prayer uttered by the sinner himself may be far more efficacious than the prayers offered up for him by others. We admit that these propositions are found in St. Chrysostom; and we add that they may be found in nearly every Catholic manual on our book-shelves. There is not a single statement in them in any way incompatible with belief in the priest's power of forgiving sin. To allege them as a proof of "inconsistency" on the part of St. Chrysostom is a revelation of ignorance on the part of the historian. No! not ignorance, I fear. Mr. Lea seems to know very well what he is writing about. He continues (p. 115):

"In other passages he [Chrysostom] exalts the power of the priesthood beyond the most extravagant claims put forward since his time. Whatever they do is confirmed by God, who ratifies the sentences of His servants ; their empire is as complete as though they were already in Heaven; it is not only in Baptism that they regenerate us, but they can pardon subsequent sins."

We need make no commentary on these words. They show quite clearly St. Chrysostom's opinion about the Power of the Keys. We will merely supplement them with the following passage from his treatise *De Sacerdotio :*

"The Jewish priests had power to cleanse the leprosy of the body, or rather not to cleanse it at all, but to decide on those who were clean, and you know what struggles there were for the sacerdotal dignity then. But these [the priests of the New Law] have received power not to cleanse the leprosy of the body but the uncleanness of the soul, *not to decide that it is cleansed, but to cleanse it absolutely;*[1] so that they who despise them are much more wicked and worthy of a greater punishment than Dathan and his associates."[2]

Our historian could not evade the express testimony of St. Ambrose and St. Chrysostom as to the priest's power of forgiving sin, except by collecting a few phrases from these great Fathers in which the power of prayer and contrition is insisted on—and then crying out, "Behold! I have made these two learned men contradict themselves!" This mode of writing history though "it may make the unskillful laugh, cannot but make the judicious grieve." But Mr. Lea, as if writing not for "the censure" of the one, but for "a whole theatre" of the others, continues:

SAINT JEROME.

"St. Jerome is less inconsequent. It is true that in one passage he speaks of the bishops as succeeding to the Apostles and as holders of the Keys of heaven, judging after a fashion before the Day of Judgment, but he qualifies this by adding that all bishops are not bishops; there was Peter but there was also Judas; it is not easy to hold the place of Peter and Paul, and the salt that

---

[1] Οὗτοι δὲ οὐ λέπραν σώματος, ἀλλ' ἀκαθαρσίαν ψυχῆς, οὐκ ἀπαλλαγεῖσαν δοκιμάζειν, ἀλλ' ἀπαλλάττειν παντελῶς ἔλαβον ἐξουσίαν.

[2] De Sacerd. Lib. III. c. 6. Migne XLVIII. 644.

has lost its savor is useless save to be cast out. Ordination evidently conferred no such power on those unworthy of it." (p. 116.)

This last sentence is a conclusion that Mr. Lea draws
from the preceding remarks of St. Jerome. The Saint
himself does not draw it. He is not so "inconsequent" as Mr. Lea thinks he is. There is nothing in
the premises that warrants such a conclusion, even
though it be true. But Mr. Lea wants it for his history
and of course he finds it.[1] He thus resumes his argument from St. Jerome (p. 116):

" In commenting moreover upon the text of Matthew
he is much more condemnatory of the claim, for he declares that bishops and priests have misinterpreted the
words of Christ and have assumed the arrogance of the
Pharisees, so they think they can condemn the innocent
and release the guilty, when in truth God only considers
the life of the sinner and not the sentence of the priests.
The only power he will allow is that of the priest in the
old law, who did not render the leper clean or unclean,
but distinguished between those who were clean and
those who were unclean. Luther himself could scarce
have said more."

If we examine carefully the passage referred to in St.
Jerome we shall see that what he censures is not the
power of remitting sin as claimed by priests, but their
arbitrary use of it. He is speaking of those who condemn the innocent and acquit the unworthy. It is not
the sentence pronounced according to the whim of the
priest—it is the life of the penitent that God is waiting
for. Again, when St. Jerome introduced the compari-

[1] S. Hieron. Epist. XIV. ad Heliod. c. 8, 9, Migne XXII. 352.

son between the priests of the Old Law and those of the New, he did so merely to show that the priests of the New Law should examine each case before pronouncing sentence. If the sinner is not in the right disposition and consequently clean, as far as his present will is considered, the priest's sentence will not make him so. Had St. Jerome intended to push the comparison so far as to establish a perfect parity between sacerdotal functions in the Old and the New Law, he would never have finished the paragraph by representing the priests of the New Law as knowing after Confession who *is to be* bound and who *is to be* loosed. The Saint would have written "scit qui *ligatus* sit quive *solutus*," but as a matter of fact, he has written "scit qui *ligandus* sit quive *solvendus*." But I must give the exact words, as they are of very great importance in determining the meaning of the previous sentences, and have been omitted by Mr. Lea. "But in accordance with his office when he [the priest and bishop] has heard the various sins, he knows who is to be bound and who is to be loosened." (Pro officio suo cum peccatorum audierit varietates, scit qui ligandus sit, quive solvendus.[1])

It is not fair to consider the words of St. Jerome apart from their conclusion or from the object that he had in view in writing them. Our historian informs us in a foot-note (p. 116), that this passage "was a stumbling block to Theologians until they concluded to ignore it." Mr. Lea, who seems so well acquainted with the Theologians may find the passage in De Lugo,[2]

[1] Com. in Matth. Lib. III. c. 16, Migne XXVI. 122.

[2] De Poen. D. XIII. sec. 2, n. 58.

Coninck,[1] Billuart,[2] Ysamberti,[3] Collet,[4] Platelli,[5] Palmieri[6] and Sasse.[7]

Theologians who omit the passage may possibly be of opinion that St. Jerome, like some of the earlier Scholastics, believed that perfect contrition is prerequired for the validity of the Sacrament of Penance, and consequently that sin is remitted before absolution and the grace accompanying it can be given.

Our historian himself must have found a stumbling block in the last part of this very same passage. St. Jerome says it is *the office* of the priest to hear the various sins (*varietates peccatorum*) of the penitent. What a telling proof for the existence of auricular and integral Confession in the early Church! Mr. Lea has ignored this statement and has not given a single reference to it in his "History of Auricular Confession." True, in speaking of private confession in the fourth century (p. 179), he briefly remarks that "St. Jerome refers to it several times." The important testimony of the Saint is summed up in this insignificant way. Two passages are indicated in a foot-note; but this passage from his commentary on St. Matthew, the most important passage of all, is quietly passed over.

After telling us how St. Jerome allows to priests no other power than was allowed them in the Old Law, our historian remarks that "Luther himself could scarce

---

[1] De Poen. D. IV. dub. 2, n. 24.

[2] De Poen. Diss. I. art. 3 § 2.   [3] De Poen. D. VIII. art. 14.

[4] Curs. Theol. Migne. Vol. XXII. p. 127.

[5] De Poen. n. 808, 809.   [6] De Poen. p. 126.   [7] De Poen. p. 45

have said more." (p. 116.)   It may be well to see what
Luther himself did say, even eleven years after he had
been excommunicated by Rome.   We have his words
in the third edition of his small Catechism—an edition
edited in Wittenberg by himself in the year 1531.

"What is Confession?   Answer:

Confession comprehends two parts: one that we confess our sins; the other that we receive absolution or
forgiveness from the father confessor, as from God himself, in nowise doubting, but firmly believing that our
sins are thereby forgiven before God in heaven." [1]

St. Jerome "himself could scarce have said more."

St. Isidore of Pelusium.

Mr. Lea resumes (p. 116):

"This shows that the priesthood were beginning
freely to claim and exercise the power of the Keys with
the inevitable abuses thence arising, of which we have
further evidence in the complaints of St. Isidore of Pelusium."

There are "inevitable abuses" connected with the
practice of law and medicine.   If Mr. Lea were writing
a history of medical practice, would he collect all the
abuses and hand them down to posterity, and say nothing about the countless benefits?   The man who would
do such a thing would be despised as the scavenger of
history.   Mr. Lea has done something very close to this
in his account of Auricular Confession.

But we must let him resume his argument from St.
Isidore:

"Priests he [Isidore] says can deprecate but not
judge.   They are mediators, not kings.   The power of

[1] Schaff, Creeds of Christendom.   Vol. III. p. 87.

the Keys comes from the Holy Ghost and is not possessed by those who are in sin, otherwise the promise
would be tyrannical and only for the benefit of priests.
Evidently the claim was gaining ground, and the power
was grasped most eagerly by those least fitted for its exercise." (p. 116.)

The question in dispute is not whether a priest un-
fitted for the power possesses it. The question is, Has
the Power of the Keys been transmitted to the priests
of the Church? and in the passage quoted from St. Isidore the question is expressly answered in the affirma-
tive. The Saint is writing to a priest who had absolved
a perjurer known to be unworthy of absolution, and he
takes occasion to insist on the idea that priests cannot
exercise this power as if it were *their own*. They are
not *kings* who can wield the power without reference to
any higher authority. They are not *judges* who can
pass sentence independently of a higher tribunal. They
are not God's colleagues. They are rather mediators,
pleaders, in a word, they are *ministers* (*ministri sunt*).
And immediately afterwards he adds, that if they possess the Holy Ghost, then they *have* the power given in
the words: "Whose sins you shall forgive they are forgiven." [1] Moreover, St. Isidore does not say that "the
promise would be tyrannical and only for the benefit of
priests," if those who are in sin possessed it. Mr. Lea
has perverted the words of the Saint. This is the exact
passage.

"If you think that this power is granted to priests,
to be exercised *when those who have sinned do not hasten*

[1] Epist. Lib. III. ep. 260. Migne Gr. LXXVIII. 941.

to atone for their sin, then this divine word [to loose—to bind] will seem to be tyrannical and to regard only the advantage of the priest and not that of those to whom an injury has been done; then also cruel and inhuman are they who exercise the function of the priesthood and do not grant pardon to everybody." (l. c.)

This passage brings out the meaning of the Saint. It is the function of the priest to pardon sin. But before he pardons thieves and robbers, restitution must be promised, else the power would be cruel and tyrannical, and most hurtful to those to whom an injury has been done. Whatever the Saint's opinion may be about unworthy priests, his opinion about the Power of the Keys is beyond cavil. Why did Mr. Lea not give us some reference to the following letter addressed by St. Isidore to the Novatian Agelides?

"In defence of your cause you have woven together trifles, composing a bitter complaint in saying that there is no force in the divine sentence which He granted to His priests for the remission of the sins of men.[1] If this is invalid, then all others are wholly uncertain, and vain is our hope, as you dogmatize."[2]

SAINT AUGUSTINE.

Let us now see what Mr. Lea has to say about St. Augustine. If St. Ambrose, St. Chrysostom and St. Jerome are guilty of inconsistencies, certainly some one must be found free from such offences. Perhaps it will be St. Augustine.

---

[1] Τὴν θείαν λέγων μὴ ἰσχύειν ἀπόφασιν, ἥνπερ τοῖς ἱερεῦσι παρέσχετο ἀφιέναι τοῖς ἀνθρωποῖς τὰ πταίσματα.

[2] Lib. L Epist. 338; Migne Gr. LXXVIII. 377.

Mr. Lea writes (p. 116):

"It was impossible that so voluminous a writer as St. Augustine, moved by varying impulses during a long series of years, should be wholly consistent in his treatment of a subject which was as yet so debatable."

Any man who cannot write a history without finding all his great authors inconsistent and self-contradictory on the question that is to form the basis of his whole work, ought to close up his books and seek for some occupation more in accord with his training and ability. But Mr. Lea continues (p. 117):

"In one of his [St. Augustine's] latest productions, reproaching the bishops and priests for the abandonment of their posts on the approach of the Vandals, he argues that it is the destruction of those who for lack of their ministrations die either un-baptized or not released from their sins. This however is probably a rhetorical amplification rather than an expression of conviction, for elsewhere his position is uniform."

"Elsewhere his position is uniform" in holding that the power of remitting sin which was granted to the Apostles was transmitted to the Church. Speaking of the man who falls into sin after baptism and foolishly refuses to change his life, he says: "Bound in the chains of sins so deadly, he refuses, delays or hesitates to fly to those Keys of the Church by which he may be loosed on earth that he may be loosed in heaven.[1] And again, referring to the Novatians, he writes: "Nor are we to listen to those who deny that the Church of God can remit all sins."[2]

[1] Serm. 351. n; 9; Migne XXXIX. 1545.
[2] De Agon. Christian. c. 31; Migne XL. 308.

But it is useless for us to quote passages from St. Augustine in favor of our view; most of those that Mr. Lea quotes for himself will prove for us.

He resumes (p. 117):

"The power granted to St. Peter was transmitted to the Church at large, which consists of the whole body of the faithful; amendment combined with faith in its power to save is all that is needed to obtain forgiveness."

In proof of this double assertion, Mr. Lea refers us to *eight* passages in St. Augustine. In the *first* of these,[1] all that we find is that Christ gave His Church the Keys, that she might loose and bind, "evidently intending that no sin should be remitted to the man who did not believe that sin could be remitted in the Church." In the *third, sixth* and *seventh* passages,[2] the Saint merely lays down the doctrine that the Church *has* the power of forgiving sin. In the *second* and *fourth* passages,[3] he says that St. Peter represented the Church when the Keys were given him. In the *fifth* passage,[4] we have only an exhortation to repentance and good works. In the *eighth*,[5] there is nothing at all about St. Peter, the Keys or the remission of post-baptismal sin. So in not one of the eight passages referred to by Mr. Lea is there

[1] De Doct. Christ. Lib. I. c. 18, Migne XXXIV. 25.

[2] Enar. in Ps. 101. Sermo 2. § 3, Migne XXXVII. 1306; De Agon. Christ. c. 31, Migne XL. 308; Enchir. c. 65, Migne XL. 262.

[3] Sermo 149, c. 6, Migne XXXVIII. 802; Sermo 295, c. 2, Migne XXXVIII. 1349.

[4] Sermo 351, c. 5, Migne XXXIX. 1548.

[5] Sermo 312, c. 3, Migne XXXVIII. 1421.

a single statement at variance with the teaching of the Catholic Church. On the contrary, in the sixth and seventh passages St. Augustine is expressly refuting the Novatian heresy, and maintains that there is no sin that the Church cannot forgive. In the second and fourth passages, where he says that St. Peter represented the Church, he explains that the representation consisted in this—that the gift was not personally bestowed on Peter so as to cease with him, but was to be transmitted to the Church. "In many places of Holy Scripture," he writes, "St. Peter appears as representing the Church, especially in that place where it is said, ' I will give to thee the Keys,' " etc. " Did Peter receive those Keys, and Paul not receive them? Did Peter receive them and John and James and the rest of the Apostles not receive them? Or are *those* Keys not in the Church where sins are daily remitted?" (Aut non sunt istæ in Ecclesia claves, ubi peccata quotidie dimittuntur?)[1] Therefore, according to St. Augustine, the Keys that St. Peter received, in as far as they regard the power of remitting sin, were received for the Church and are still in the Church. If *those* same Keys are in the Church they must be administered by individuals as they were in the days of the Apostles. To talk of the Keys being administered by the Church *at large* is to put a meaning (and a fantastic one) on the words of St. Augustine that the Saint never dreamed of. Such phrases as: "The Keys were granted to the Church," "The Church has the power of remitting sin" meant

[1] Sermo 149, c. 6, Migne XXXVIII. 802.

for St. Augustine, as they mean to-day in every Catholic
book of theology, that the Power of the Keys was
granted to the Church, and is exercised by the Church
through her *duly appointed ministers.* In one of the very
sermons referred to by Mr. Lea in his eight references,
this doctrine is expressly laid down by St. Augustine
himself. Speaking of the repentant sinner he says :
"Let him come to the priests by whom those Keys are
administered for him in the Church." (Veniat ad an-
tistites per quos illi in Ecclesia claves ministrantur.)[1]

"In combating the Donatists who assumed that the
power was personal to the priest he argues that this is
fatuous and heretical. Christ had said, 'Thy faith hath
made thee whole,' and now man presumes to do what
Christ as a man had refrained from doing and arrogates
the power to himself." (Lea, p. 117.)

St. Augustine was quite right in putting down as
fatuous and heretical an opinion that claimed the power
to forgive sin as the *personal* power of man. It is not
man's power that grants remission. Even Christ would
not assert the power as long as He was reputed mere
man. It is God's power acting through man. St.
Augustine explains his meaning very clearly in his
treatise against the Donatist, Parmenian, when he draws
a distinction between *ab hominibus* and *per homines.*
The former as seeming to denote *principal* causality he
sets aside, the latter as implying *instrumental* causality
he admits and defends. He then adds that the words
"receive ye the Holy Ghost," show that it is not men
who remit sin "but the Holy Ghost *through them,* as the

---

[1] Sermo 351, n. 9, Migne XXXIX. 1545.

Gospel says in another place: 'It is not you that speak, but the spirit of your Father that speaketh in you.' "
(*Satis ostenditur non ipsos id agere sed per eos utique Spiritum Sanctum, sicut alio loco dicit,* "*Non enim vos estis qui loquimini sed Spiritus Sanctus qui in vobis est.*")[1] The ministerial power of the priest to remit sin could not be more pithily expressed or more beautifully illustrated.

Mr. Lea resumes:

"The passage in John (xx. 22-3) he [St. Augustine] explains as meaning that the charity of the Church diffused in our hearts by the Holy Ghost dismisses the sins of those sharing it, and retains them in those who do not share it." (p. 117.)

Mr. Lea means that in one place St. Augustine concludes from the words in John [xx. 22–3] that the infused virtue of Charity which comes from the Holy Ghost, and is to be had only in the Church, remits mortal sin. We have no objection to urge against this doctrine. The question is, Through what instrumentality is Charity or Sanctifying Grace produced in the soul? St. Augustine's deduction from the text of St. John is wholly irrelevant to the present controversy.[2]

"Yet with all his learning and acuteness St. Augustine had the vaguest possible conception of what was the nature of this mysterious power to bind and to loose." (Lea, p. 118.)

St. Augustine, who is very frank in acknowledging difficulties and obscurities in Scripture, nowhere tells us that his conception was "the vaguest possible"

[1] Contra Epist. Parmen. Lib. II. c. 24; Migne XLIII. 67.
[2] In Joan. Trac. 121, n. 4, Migne XXXV. 1958.

about the power of "loosing and binding." Mr. Lea
in finding fault with the "vagueness" of St. Augustine,
is somewhat like the young dialectician who finds fault
with the "vagueness" of Aristotle. If this however
were the only difficulty, we might possibly pardon Mr.
Lea, but the following passage seems to reveal him in
another character.

He says (p. 118):

"In one place he [St. Augustine] explains it [the
power of loosing and binding] by the judgments rendered by the martyrs who are to sit on thrones during
the Millennium."

On examining this passage I find, 1. St. Augustine
understands by the Millennium, the *present* age of the
Church. 2. He is speaking of the souls of the Martyrs
as reigning with Christ inasmuch as they still belong to
His Kingdom. 3. He nowhere says that the Martyrs
have the power of "loosing or binding." 4. He expressly states that this power of "loosing and binding"
is exercised by the Authorities by whom the Church is
at present governed. Here is a literal translation of the
passage:

"It is then of this kingdom militant, in which conflict with the enemy is still maintained, and war carried
on with warring lusts, or government laid upon them
as they yield, until we come to that most peaceful
kingdom in which we shall reign without an enemy,
and it is of this *first resurrection* in the *present life* that the
Apocalypse speaks in the words just quoted. For after
saying that the devil is bound a thousand years and is
afterwards loosed for a short season, it goes on to give
a sketch of what the Church does or of what is done in
the Church in those days, in the words, 'And I saw

seats and them that sat upon them, and judgment was given.' It is not to be supposed that this refers to the last judgment, but to the seats of *the rulers* and the *rulers themselves by whom the Church is now governed*. (*Sedes praepositorum, et ipsi praepositi intelligendi sunt per quos Ecclesia nunc gubernatur.*) And no better interpretation of judgment being given can be produced than that which we have in the words, 'What ye bind on earth shall be bound in heaven; and what ye loose on earth shall be loosed in heaven.'"[1]

Almost immediately after this quotation from the Gospel, St. Augustine resumes the words of the Apocalypse (xx. 4): "And the souls of them that were slain for the testimony of Jesus and for the word of God," and he tells us that this part of the text must be understood with the words that follow, viz.: "they reigned with Christ a thousand years." From this, the Saint goes on to show how "the souls of the pious dead" are still united with the Church and in this sense reign with Christ as the years run on. Nowhere in the passage does he say that the souls of the Martyrs exercise the power of "loosing and binding." On the contrary, he claims this power for the rulers of the Church; not for "the Church at large"—it should be remarked—but for those who *govern* the Church. Why did Mr. Lea not call attention to this last statement? It is a direct contradiction of what he imputes to the Saint in a previous passage. However, such an omission might possibly be condoned as an oversight, but there is no condonation for juggling with the words of St. Augustine

[1] Edin. Trans. Vol. II. p. 365. De Civ. Dei. Lib. XX. c. 9, Migne XLI. 673.

and putting the souls of Martyrs on seats which, according to the Saint, are occupied by Bishops. Some one considered it a joke to unite the texts: "Judas went out and hanged himself," "Go thou and do likewise." Mr. Lea has actually perpetrated a combination of almost the same kind, but in dead earnest and without the justification of a joke.

But we will let him continue his argument from St. Augustine.

"Again in praying for the conversion of the Manichæans he assumes that conversion and repentance will win remission of their sins and blasphemies, and if he refers casually to the power of the Keys lodged in the Church, it is apparently only to indicate that by Baptism in the Church they will be in a position to obtain pardon." (p. 118.)

Sacerdotal absolution is given only for sins committed after Baptism. Mr. Lea seems to imply that if it were in use it would be given to the Manichæans on their reception into the Church. Hence he is disappointed, or feigns to be, at not finding St. Augustine praying for the absolution of the Manichæans. St. Augustine prayed for their conversion and Baptism. Mr. Lea, I suppose, had he believed in such things, would have prayed for their future Absolution and subsequent Extreme Unction.

"And yet again he [Augustine] argues that through the Keys the Church has the power of inflicting punishment worse than death by the sword, by fire or by beasts, though the individual priest has no power; God pardons or condemns wholly irrespective of what the priest may say or do." (Lea, p. 118.)

Yes, St. Augustine says that "through the Keys the
Church has the power of inflicting punishment worse
than death by the sword, by fire or by beasts," but he
does not limit the assertion by saying that "the individual priest has no power."[1] This is an addition made
by Mr. Lea. Again, our historian makes St. Augustine
assert, that "God pardons or condemns wholly irrespective of what the priest may say or do." In confirmation of this statement we find at the foot of the
page the very words of the Saint. But Mr. Lea has
omitted two phrases in the middle of the passage that
show quite clearly, even apart from the context, that
St. Augustine says something absolutely different from
what Mr. Lea's rendering of the text implies. The
Saint is speaking of thieves, adulterers and voluptuaries
who put off repentance from day to day, (*mores suos non
mutantibus*). Then he adds : "The Lord threatens
them with death, he threatens them with hell, he
threatens them with eternal destruction. What do
they wish? That I promise them what He does not
promise them? Behold the procurator grants thee security: what does it profit thee if the Master of the
house does not accept it? *I am the procurator, I am the
servant: dost thou want me to say to thee: 'Live as thou
pleasest, the Lord will not destroy thee?'*[2] The procurator
has given thee security: the security of the procurator
profits nothing. Would that the Lord would give it to
thee, and that I could make thee solicitous. The secur-

---

[1] Contra Advers. Legis, § 36, Migne XLII. 623.

[2] The words in italics have been omitted by Mr. Lea.

ity of the Lord is of value, even though I wish it not; mine is of no value if He wishes it not." [1]

This is a beautiful exposition of Catholic doctrine. The priest is the Lord's procurator, and is therefore employed to act for the Lord. As long as he acts according to his Master's will, his action is valid; if he acts in opposition to that will and grants anything to the undeserving, his action is null and void.

In going to the "original sources" to which Mr. Lea refers us, we find not only nothing against Catholic doctrine, but, as a rule, some of the most beautiful illustrations and arguments in its favor. He told us in his preface that he himself was going to the "original sources." If he went, then his book makes us hang down our heads for the frailty of human nature.

From the "original sources" we could have brought forth many other striking arguments in favor of the Catholic doctrine if our object had been to write a history of the Keys during the first five centuries of Christianity. But our object has been to destroy, not to build up. We have written these pages merely to show to Catholics the kind of an adversary, and to Protestants the kind of a champion, that they have in Mr. Lea.

We have examined, line for line, ten pages of his first volume. We think that our readers will consider it useless to carry the examination any further. The question that Mr. Lea has been treating in this section is the vital question of the whole work; and nevertheless what false assumptions, what unwarranted conclu-

[1] Sermo 40, c. 5, Migne XXXVIII. 246.

sions, what suppressions of truth, what perverted representations of patristic teaching, in a word, what methods of the special pleader have we not discovered in his pages? Mr. Lea is not a historian, but an advocate; a writer not of history, but of polemics. He writes to prove a thesis, to gain a cause, to misrepresent an adversary. He summons up his witnesses from antiquity, good and bad alike, heretic or orthodox, all are acceptable if only they may be coerced into an utterance to suit his purpose. If they utter nothing at all, their silence is construed into evident testimony in favor of his cause. If they prove recalcitrant and are bent on giving evidence against him, then he tries to show that they are "inconsistent." These are not the methods of the great men who write history. They are not the methods of any writer who wants to have the truth known. They are the methods of a man whose object in life seems to be to discredit Catholicity and to mislead those outside the Catholic Church as to the belief of their Fathers in the Faith. And what aggravates the pain for those who think over the matter is, that all this is done in the name and disguise of History.

WOODSTOCK COLLEGE,
   WOODSTOCK,
     MARYLAND.

APPENDIX.

THAT Mr. Lea's own text and references may be seen, we subjoin an exact reprint of his preface and of the pages examined in this little book. As there is nothing to our purpose on page 107 except three texts of Scripture and a foot-note, we take the liberty of not reproducing the entire page.

(80)

PREFACE.

Perhaps in treating the subject of the present work I may be accused of threshing old straw. For nearly four centuries it has served as material for endless controversy, and its every aspect may be thought to have been exhausted. Yet I have sought to view it from a different standpoint and to write a history, not a polemical treatise. With this object I have abstained from consulting Protestant writers and have confined myself exclusively to the original sources and to Catholic authorities, confident that what might thus be lost in completeness would be compensated by accuracy and impartiality. In this I have not confined myself to standard theological treatises, but have largely referred to popular works of devotion in which is to be found the practical application of the theories enunciated by the masters of theology. I have purposely been sparing of comment, preferring to present facts and to leave the reader to draw his own conclusions.

I may perhaps be pardoned for the hope that, in spite of the arid details of which such an investigation as this must in part consist, the reader may share in the human interest which has vitalized the labor for me in tracing the gradual growth and development of a system that has, in a degree unparalleled elsewhere, subjected the intellect and conscience of successive generations to the domination of fellow mortals. The history of mankind may be vainly searched for another institution which has established a spiritual autocracy such as that of the Latin Church, or which has exercised so vast an influence on human destinies, and it has seemed to me a service to historical truth to examine somewhat minutely into the origin and

development of the sources of its power. This can only be done
intelligently by the collocation of a vast aggregate of details, many
of them apparently trivial, but all serving to show how, amid the
clash of contending opinions, the structure gradually arose which
subjugated Christendom beneath its vast and majestic omnipotence,
profoundly affecting the course of European history and moulding
in no small degree the conception of the duties which man owes to
his fellows and to his God. Incidentally, moreover, the investigation affords a singularly instructive example of the method of
growth of dogma, in which every detail once settled becomes the
point of departure in new and perhaps wholly unexpected directions.

The importance of the questions thus passed in review is by no
means limited to the past, for in the Latin Church spiritual inter-
ests cannot be dissociated from temporal. The publicist must be
singularly blind who fails to recognize the growth of influence that
has followed the release of the Holy See from the entanglements
consequent upon its former position as a petty Italian sovereign, and
the enormous opportunities opened to it by the substitution of the
rule of the ballot-box for absolutism. Through the instrumentality
of the confessional, the sodality and the indulgence, its matchless
organization is thus enabled to concentrate in the Vatican a power
greater than has ever before been wielded by human hands.

Philadelphia, December, 1895.

" And I will give to thee [Peter] the keys of the kingdom of heaven. And whatsoever thou shalt bind on earth, it shall be bound also in heaven: and whatsoever thou shalt loose on earth it shall be loosed also in heaven " (Matt. xvi. 19).

" Amen I say to you, whatsoever you shall bind upon earth shall be bound also in heaven ; and whatsoever you shall loose upon earth shall be loosed also in heaven " (Matt. xviii. 18).

" Receive ye the Holy Ghost. Whose sins you shall forgive, they are forgiven them; and whose sins you shall retain, they are retained " (John xx. 22-23).[1]

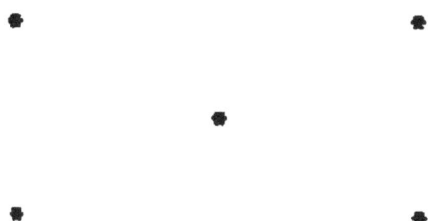

---

[1] The orthodox explanation of the reiteration of the grant of power by Christ, after his resurrection, is that in Matthew he merely made a promise, the fulfilment of which is recorded in John.

Even admitting that the texts have the sense ascribed to them by the Church,

Whatever sense may be attributed to this grant of power, the primitive Church evidently regarded it as personal to the holy men whom Christ had selected as his immediate representatives. At the time the gospels were composed the apostles were not expected to have any successors, for Christ had foretold the coming of the Day of Judgment before that generation should pass away,[1] and the presence of this in all the synoptic gospels shows how universal among Christians was the expectation of its fulfilment. In fact, how slowly the idea was developed that even the apostles had this power is seen in Philip's referring Simon Magus to God for forgiveness after repentance[2] and in the legend related above from Eusebius of St. John and the robber. Had the belief existed the apostle would not have been represented as offering his own soul in exchange and as interceding long and earnestly with God: as soon as assured of the sinner's repentance he would have been recorded as absolving him. The early Christians would have stood aghast at the suggestion that God would confer such awful authority on every vicious or ignorant man who through favor or purchase might succeed in obtaining ordination. That such a pretension should be accepted by Europe, even in the Dark Ages, would be incredible if it had not proved a fact. The transmission of the power from the apostles to those who were

---

there is a serious deficiency in the grant, for they do not say that no sins shall be remitted save those pardoned by the Apostles; the power must be exercised to be effective, and a sinner may make his peace with God otherwise. The point is of no importance save as affording an illustration of the boundless assumptions by which Catholic teachers maintain the power of the keys. Thus Palmieri (Tract. de Pœnitent. p 102) asserts that the Apostles bind whomsoever they do not loose—"Apostoli autem tamdiu retinent quamdiu non absolvunt," and he even has the audacity to represent Christ as saying "independenter a ministerio Apostolico nolo remitti quodlibet peccatum."

Equally audacious was the attempt made in 1625 by the Jesuit Santarel to prove that the text in Matthew was not confined to the forum of conscience but that it gave the Church and the pope supreme temporal power over all rulers (D'Argentré, Collect. judic. de novis Erroribus II. II. 213). Bellarmine reaches the same result, but by a different process (De Controversiis Christianæ Fidei, Cont. III. Lib. v. c. 6) and it was the received Jesuit doctrine. See La Theologie Morale des Jésuites (Ant. Arnauld), Cologne, 1667, pp. 121 sqq.

[1] Matt. XXIV. 34; Mark XIII. 30; Luke XXI. 32.

[2] Acts VIII. 22. This did not escape Wickliffe in his controversies over the power of the keys. See Thomas of Walden's De Sacramentis c. CXLV. n. 2.

assumed to be their successors is the most audacious *non sequitur* in history, and the success of the attempt can scarce be overestimated as a factor in the development of religion and civilization.[1]

That the primitive Church knew nothing of this is plainly inferable from the silence of the early Fathers. It is proverbially difficult to prove a negative, and in this case the only evidence is negative. They could not discuss or oppose a non-existent doctrine and practice and their only eloquence on the subject must perforce be silence, but as they treated earnestly on the methods of obtaining pardon for sins, their omission of all allusion to any power of remission lodged in priest or Church is perfectly incompatible with the existence of contemporaneous belief in it. We have seen already (Chapter I.) that St. Clement of Rome, the Didache, Barnabas, St. Ignatius and the Shepherd of Hermas, while counselling sinners as to reconciliation with God, know nothing of any authority under God. St. Ignatius, who magnified the episcopal office, speaks indeed of the council of the bishop (p. 6) as an element, but ascribes to him no individual power. Irenæus asks how sins can be remitted unless God against whom we have sinned remits them to us[2] and evidently is ignorant of any intermediary function. St. Dionysius of Corinth orders all returning sinners to be received back kindly and says nothing about absolving them.[3] The Epistle of St. Polycarp to the Philippians is a summary exhortation as to conduct and practice in which, if confession and absolution were customary or recognized, he could not avoid referring to them, but he says nothing about

---

[1] When Luther, who followed his master St. Augustin in holding that the power of the keys was lodged in the Church at large, argued that otherwise there would be no reply to the heretics who asserted that the gift was personal to Peter and died with him, the only answer which his antagonist Faber deigned to make was that there are no heretics so foolish as to make an assertion so futile and shadowy, and with this he declares that the whole of Luther's position is swept away.—Joh. Fabri Opus adversus nova Dogmata Lutheri, Romæ, 1522, H. i].

Faber was a Dominican Humanist, allied with Erasmus, Zwingli and other early reformers until alarmed at the progress of the Reformation he became one of its most active and efficient opponents. His book won him much applause in Rome; he became bishop of Vienna, where he manifested his zeal by earnest labors to reform his clergy and also by procuring the burning of Balthasar Hubmeier, March 10, 1528.

[2] Irenæi contra Hæreses Lib. v. c. xvii. §§1, 2.

[3] Euseb. H. E. iv. 23.

them. Nor in the paragraph as to the duties of priests is there any
allusion to such functions or to mediation between God and man.
As for the priest Valens and his wife, who had misbehaved he only
says, "May God grant them true repentance!" The whole epistle
pictures a church of the utmost simplicity, in which man deals directly with his Creator.[1] In fact the custom which prevailed, as
we have seen, of not admitting clerics to penance shows that the
whole penitential system had nothing to do with the relations between the sinner and his God.

The first allusion to any power of pardoning sin occurs early in
the third century, when Tertullian protested vigorously on hearing
that it was proposed at Rome to remit the sin of fornication and
adultery to those who had duly performed penance.[2] Whether this
purpose was carried out or not we have no means of knowing positively, but there is every appearance that the project was allowed to
drop as there is no trace in any subsequent document that adultery
was treated with greater mildness than homicide or idolatry—indeed, we have seen that in some African churches those guilty of it
were not even received to penitence. Yet that the subject was
beginning to attract attention and provoke discussion is shown by
Tertullian's argument that the grant to Peter was personal; the
apostles had the power of forgiving sins, and this has been transmitted to the Church; if the bishop of Rome claims it, let him
show his right by performing miracles like the apostles.[3]

The idea gradually made its way in some churches, though under
varying conditions. Not long after Tertullian the canons of Hippolytus, in the ritual of episcopal ordination, show that God was
prayed to bestow on the bishop the power of remitting sins,[4] and the

---

[1] S. Polycarp. Epist. ad Philippenses.

[2] Audio etiam edictum esse propositum et quidem peremptorium Pontifex
scilicet maximus quod et episcopus episcoporum edicit ' Ego et mœchiæ et
fornicationis delicta pœnitentia functis dimitto."—Tertull. de Pudicit. c. 1.

[3] Ibid. c. 21.

[4] Tribue etiam illi O Domine episcopatum et spiritum clementem et potestatem ad remittenda peccata.—Canon. Hippolyti III. 17.

This was not the only supernatural gift which the superstition of the age
ascribed to the episcopal office. As the shadow of Peter cured the sick, Acts
v. 15 was made the basis of a claim, as well as Matt. xvi. 19, that the bishop
was held to be able to relieve disease. The prayer of ordination adds "et
tribue ei facultatem ad dissolvenda omnia vincula iniquitatis dæmonum et ad

Apostolic Constitutions, based on these canons, have nearly the same formula at the close of the third century.[1] How completely dependent on local usage however was this claim is seen in the ordination of priests. In the Canons of Hippolytus the same prayer was used for them as for bishops; in an Egyptian Ordo based on the canons, the prayer for the priest has no allusion to the remission of sins, and the same is observable in the Apostolic Constitutions.[2]

Thus in some churches the bishops were claiming the power of the keys, but in others their pretentions were ridiculed. Origen tells us that they cited the text in Matthew as though they held the power to bind and to loose; this is well, if they can perform the works for which Christ made the grant to Peter, but it is absurd in him who is bound in the chains of his own sins to pretend to loosen others, simply because he is called a bishop.[3] Evidently to Origen ordination conferred no such power; to him the priest was a mediator who propitiated God at the altar.[4] We have already seen that Cyprian disclaimed all power to absolve; the Church could condemn by refusing reconciliation, but those whom it admitted to peace were only referred to the judgment of God to confirm or annul the decision. In another passage he is even more emphatic. Let no one, he says,

---

sanandos omnes morbos et contere Satanam sub pedibus ejus." This was accomplished by a visit and a prayer of the bishop—" Magna enim res est infirmo a principe sacerdotum visitari; quia umbra Petri sanavit infirmum" (Ibid. xxiv. 199). See also Irenæi contra Hæreses, ii. 32-4 and Tertull. ad Scapulam c. 4. It was a common belief that sickness was caused by demons and that driving them away ensured recovery (Tatiani contra Græcos Oratio). The canons of Hippolytus do not cite Mark xvi. 17-18, which is more to the purpose, probably because the conclusion of that gospel as we have it was unknown at the time.

[1] Da ei Domine omnipotens per Christum tuum participationem sancti Spiritus ut habeat potestatem dimittendi peccata secundum mandatum tuum (κατὰ τὴν ἐντολήν σου)."—Constitt. Apostol. Lib. viii. c. 3. It is worth while to remark the deprecatory character of these rituals in contrast with the indicative form of the later " Accipe Spirtum sanctum."

[2] Achelis, Die Canones Hippolyti, pp. 61-2.—Constitt. Apost. viii. 24.

[3] Alloquin ridiculum est ut dicamus eum qui vinculis peccatorum suorum ligatus est, trahit peccata sua sicut funem longum et tanquam juge lorum vituli iniquitates suas, propter hoc solum quoniam episcopus dicitur, habere hujusmodi potestatem ut soluti ab eo sint soluti in coelo aut ligati in terris sint ligati in coelo."—Origenis Comment. in Matt. Tom. xii. § 14.

[4] Origenis in Levit. Hom. vii. n. 2.

deceive himself, for none but Christ can pardon; man is not greater than God, nor can the servant condone an offence committed against his master. The most that he will admit is that the intercession of priest and martyr may incline God to mercy and change the sentence. It is the height of arrogance for man to assume that he can do what God did not concede even to the apostles—to separate the grain from the chaff and the wheat from the tares.[1] A phrase of Cyprian's contemporary, St. Firmilian of Cappadocia, has been quoted as asserting the power of the keys, but it occurs in his furious letter to Pope Stephen on the rebaptism of heretics and refers only to the remission of sin in baptism;[2] that Firmilian made no claim for such power is shown by his assembling a council in support of Novatianus.[3] Commodianus, in his instructions to penitents, says nothing of any priestly ministrations; as he had himself endured a course of penance he had every opportunity of knowing that the sinner dealt directly with God; nor in his remarks to priests and bishops does he make any allusion to their possession of such authority.[4] St. Peter of Alexandria, in 305, in his instructions for the reconciliation of those who had lapsed in the persecution of Diocletian, knows nothing of any power to remit sin; the Church can only pray that Christ may intercede for sinners with the Father.[5]

---

[1] Nemo se fallat, nemo se decipiat. Solus Dominus misereri potest. Veniam peccatis quæ in ipsum commissa sunt solus potest ille largiri qui peccata nostra portavit, qui pro nobis doluit, quem Deus tradidit pro peccatis nostris. Homo Deo esse non potest major; nec remittere aut donare indulgentia sua servus potest quod in dominum delicto graviore commissum est.—S. Cyprian. de Lapsis n. 17. Cf. n. 18, 29; Epist. 4, 55, 56; De Unitate Ecclesiæ.

Potest ille [Deus] indulgentiam dare, sententiam suam potest ille deflectere . . . potest in acceptum referre quidquid pro talibus et petierint martyres et fecerint sacerdotes.—De Lapsis n. 36.

Tum deinde quantus arrogantiæ tumor est, quanta humilitatis et lenitatis oblivio, arrogantiæ suæ quanta jactatio ut quis aut audeat aut facere se posse credat, quod nec apostolis concessit Dominus, ut zizania a frumento putet se posse decernere, aut quasi ipsi palam ferre et aream purgare concessum sit, paleas conetur a tritico separare.—Epist. 55.

[2] Cypriani Epist. 75 (Ed. Oxon). It is somewhat remarkable to find this abusive epistle quoted by a Catholic, as Binterim does (Denkwürdigkeiten Bd. V. Th. ii. p. 183) and to see it moreover cooly attributed to Cyprian himself.

[3] Euseb. H. E. vi. 44.   [4] Commodiani Instructiones, n. 49, 69.

[5] S. Petri Alexandr. Can. xi.

Yet when a claim such as that inferred in the ordination ritual of the Canons of Hippolytus had once been made, it was sure, in the plastic condition of doctrine and practice, to develop with the increasing power and pretensions of the Church as it emerged from persecution to domination. Appetite grows by what it feeds on and it would have required abnegation not often predicable of human nature for bishops not to grasp at such authority after it had been advanced and exercised by a few. There is a hint of this in the remark of the Novatian Bishop Acesius who attended the council of Nicæa and subscribed to its canons but refused to join in communion with his fellow members, and when asked by Constantine the reason replied that he considered those unworthy of communion who would admit to the sacraments a man who had sinned since baptism, for such remission of sin depended on the power of God and not on the will of a priest, whereupon the emperor said to him "Acesius, get a ladder and go up to heaven by yourself."[1] Still the development of the power of the keys was wonderfully slow. As Lactantius was not a priest but a philosopher, his testimony on such a subject does not count for much, but he knows nothing of the priest as an intermediary; the sinner deals directly with God.[2] St. Hilary of Poitiers is a more significant witness, and in his Commentary on Matthew he seems ignorant of the claim that the power of binding and loosing was conferred on the apostles to be transmitted to their successors. He treats it wholly as a personal grant to them and makes no allusion to any other view of the matter.[3] Various other writers of the second half of the fourth century ascribe no pardoning power to the Church; the fate of the sinner depends exclusively on God.[4] St.

---

[1] Sozomen. H. E. I. 22. There is something of the same to be gathered from the conference between Atticus Bishop of Constantinople and Asclepiades, the Novatian Bishop of Nicæa.—Socrat. H. E. VII. 25.

[2] Lactant. Divin. Institt. Lib. IV. c. 17; Lib. VI. c. 13, 24.

[3] S. Hilarii Pictav. Comment in Matt. c. XVI. n. 7; c. XVIII. n. 8. Possibly his assertion that the Pharisees claimed to hold the keys of heaven (c. XII. n. 3) may have been intended as a covert rebuke to the high sacerdotalists. Juenin (De Sacram. Diss. VI. Q. V. Cap. 1 Art. 2 § 2) admits that Hilary does not claim the power as transmitted to the successors of the apostles, but Palmieri (Tract. de Pœnit. p. 114) boldly quotes what he says as to the apostolic power, as though he conceded the transmission.

[4] Philastrii Lib. de Hæres. n. 84.—Marii Victorini in Epist. ad Ephes. Lib. I. n. 7.—S. Epiphanii Panar. Hæres. 59.

Pacianus, when controverting the Novatians, asserts that the power
of the keys was transmitted to the successors of the apostles, to be
exercised with the utmost caution and only in accordance with the
Divine will, but this was a mere speculative argument, for in his
exhortation to sinners he only ascribes to the Church a power to
assist, and it is Christ who obtains pardon for us.[1] The Manichæans seem to have been the first to discover the power of the
keys. Their elect could not handle money and when in want of
food would undertake to remit sins for bread. Ephraim Syrus denounces them bitterly for this; there is but One who can remit sins,
except in the rite of baptism.[2] Possibly this example may have begun to infect the Church, for his contemporary, St. Basil the Great,
claims that authority to bind and to loose is lodged with the bishops.[3]

It is highly probable in fact that the Novatian schism stimulated
greatly the progress of sacerdotalism against which it was a protest.
The schismatics doubtless did not forego the advantage offered them
by the hazy and dubious character of the *pax ecclesiæ* which the
priests conferred and contemptuously asked what was after all the
advantage of the reconciliation purchased at so heavy a cost, and
the orthodox in answering them would naturally be led to exalt the
efficacy of its redeeming power and to assert that it was equivalent to
divine pardon. This process is well illustrated by the contradictory
utterances of St. Ambrose. Stimulated by conflict with the Novatians,
in some passages he asserts the power of the keys in the hands of
bishops in an unqualified manner; Christ, he says, could remove sin

[1] S. Paciani contra Novatianos Epist. I.—Paranæsis ad Pœnitentiam.—
"Qui fratribus peccata sua non tacet, ecclesiæ lacrymis adjutus, Christi pre-
cibus absolvitur."

[2] Wegnern Manichæorum Indulgentiæ pp. 187-88 (Lipsiæ, 1827).—"Canes
morbidi sunt qui, cum panis buccellas non inveniant, peccata et debita re-
mittunt. Qua in re admodum rabiosi sunt et digni qui contundantur; quum
unus tantum qui peccantibus peccata remittere posset."

It is generally assumed that St. Maximus of Turin (Homil. CIV.) in the latter half of the century is describing the Manichæans when he speaks of the
invasion of the land by heretics whose priests sell pardon of sin for money,
and say "Pro crimine da tantum mihi et indulgetur tibi. Vanus plane et
insipiens presbyter, qui cum ille prædam accipiat putat quod peccatum
Christus indulgeat." St. Maximus could hardly have anticipated the time
when, as we shall see hereafter, the teaching which he thus denounced was
practiced by pardoners in all the lands of the Roman obedience.

[3] S. Basil. Epist. Canon. III. c. 74.

by a word, but he has ordered that it should be done through men.[1]
Thus he pushes this to an extent so insane that he represents God
as wishing to be asked to pardon and as virtually unable to do so
without the action of the priest.[2] In cooler moments he assumes
that this power is lodged in the Church at large, and limits it to
intercessory prayer denying that the priest can exercise any power;[3]
and when it came to the practical exertion of the power he denies
that he possesses it and attributes it solely to God,[4] while his biographer Paulinus tells us that he regarded himself merely as an intercessor.[5] The same inconsistency is found in Chrysostom. We
have seen how he assumes that pardon is to be had by almsgiving
and other good works. Elsewhere he emphatically declares that
no intercessor is needed; God freely forgives those who seek him
with heartfelt tears; the prayer of the wicked is much more efficacious with God than any intercessory prayers can be.[6] In other
passages he exalts the power of the priesthood beyond the most extravagant claims put forward since his time. Whatever they do is confirmed by God, who ratifies the sentences of his servants; their empire
is as complete as though they were already in heaven; it is not only
in baptism that they regenerate us, but they can pardon subsequent

---

[1] S. Ambros. in Ps. CXVIII. Serm. x. n. 17.—In Ps. XXXVIII. Enarrat. n. 37,
38.—Exposit. Evangel. sec. Lucam Lib. v. Serm. 10 n. 13.—De Cain et Abel
Lib. II. c. iv. n. 15.—De Pœnitent. Lib. I. c. 7, 8.

[2] Quis enim tu es qui Domino contradicas, ne cui velit culpam relaxat, cum
tu cui volueris ignoscas? Vult rogari, vult obsecrari. Si omnium justitia,
ubi Dei gratiæ? Quis es tu qui invideas Domino?—Exposit. Evangel. sec.
Lucam Lib. VII. n. 235-6.

[3] De Pœnitent. Lib. I. c. 2.—Exposit. Evangel. sec. Lucam Lib. v. Serm x.
n. 11, 92; Lib. VII. n. 225.—In Ps. XXXVIII. Enarrat, n. 10.—De Spiritu Sancto
Lib. III. c. xviii. n. 137.

[4] In his well-known letter to Theodosius St. Ambrose says, "Peccatum non
tollitur nisi lacrymis et pœnitentia. Nec Angelus potest nec archangelus:
Dominus ipse qui solus potest dicere *Ego vobiscum sum*, si peccaverimus nisi
pœnitentiam deferentibus non relaxat."—S. Ambros. Epist. LI. c. 11.

[5] Paulini Vit. S. Ambros. c. 39.

[6] Nam ipse solus cordi medelam afferre potest . . . sine intercessore exor-
abilis est, sine pecuniis sine sumptibus petitioni annuit: sufficit solo corde
clamare et lacrymas offerre et statim ingressus eum attraxeris.—S. Joh. Chrysost. de Pœnit. Homil. IV. § 4. Cf. Homil. VIII. § 2.—In Epist. ad Hebræos
Homil. IX. § 4.—Homil. XI. non hactenus editæ Hom. VI.—Homil. in Philip-
pens. I. 18.

sins.[1] St. Jerome is less inconsequent. It is true that in one passage he speaks of the bishops as succeeding to the Apostles and, as holders of the keys of heaven, judging after a fashion before the Day of Judgment, but he qualifies this by adding that all bishops are not bishops; there was Peter but also there was Judas; it is not easy to hold the place of Peter and Paul, and the salt that has lost its savor is useless save to be cast out.[2] Ordination evidently conferred no power on those unworthy of it. In commenting, moreover, upon the text of Matthew he is much more condemnatory of the claim, for he declares that bishops and priests have misinterpreted the words of Christ and have assumed the arrogance of the Pharisees, so they think that they can condemn the innocent and release the guilty, when in truth God only considers the life of the sinner and not the sentence of the priests. The only power he will allow is that of the priest in the old law, who did not render the leper clean or unclean, but distinguished between those who were clean and those who were unclean.[3] Luther himself could scarce have said more.

This shows that the priesthood were beginning freely to claim and exercise the power of the keys, with the inevitable abuses thence arising, of which we have further evidence in the complaints of St. Isidor of Pelusium. Priests he says can deprecate but not judge, they are mediators, not kings. The power of the keys comes from the Holy Ghost and is not possessed by those who are in sin, otherwise the promise would be tyrannical and only for the benefit of priests.[4] Evidently the claim was gaining ground and the power naturally was grasped most eagerly by those least fitted for its exercise.

It was impossible that so voluminous a writer as St. Augustin, moved by varying impulses during a long series of years, should be

---

[1] S. Joh. Chrysost. de Sacerdotio Lib. III. c. 5, 6.--" Neque enim tantum cum nos regenerant [aqua baptismi] sed etiam post regenerationem admissa peccata condonare possunt."

[2] S. Hieron. Epist. xiv. ad Heliodor. c. 8, 9.

[3] Istum locum [Matt. xvi. 19] episcopi et presbyteri non intelligentes aliquid sibi de Pharisæorum assumunt supercilio, ut vel damnent innocentes vel solvere se noxios arbitrentur: cum apud Deum non sententia sacerdotum sed reorum vita quæratur.—S. Hieron. Comment. in Evangel. Matthæi Lib. III. c. xvi. v. 19. We shall see hereafter what a stumbling-block was this passage to the theologians until they concluded to ignore it.

[4] S. Isidori Pelusiot. Lib. III. Epis. 260.—Ministri enim sunt, non participes, deprecatores non judices, mediatores non reges."

wholly consistent in his treatment of a subject which was as yet so debatable. In one of his latest productions, reproaching the bishops and priests for the abandonment of their posts on the approach of the Vandals, he argues that it is the destruction of those who for lack of their ministrations die either unbaptized or not released from their sins.[1] This however is probably rather a rhetorical amplification than an expression of conviction, for elsewhere his position is uniform. The power granted to St. Peter was transmitted to the Church at large which consists of the whole body of the faithful; amendment combined with faith in its power to save is all that is needed to obtain forgiveness.[2] In combating the Donatists, who assumed that the power was personal in the priest, he argues that this is fatuous and heretical. Christ had said "Thy faith hath made thee whole" and now man presumes to do what Christ as a man had refrained from doing, and arrogates the power to himself.[3] The passage in John (xx. 22-3) he explains as meaning that the charity of the Church diffused in our hearts by the Holy Ghost dismisses the sins of those

---

[1] Ubi si ministri desint quantum exitium sequitur eos qui de isto seculo vel non regenerati exeunt aut ligati.—S. Augustin. Epist. ccxviii. n. 8 ad Honoratum.

[2] After quoting Matt. xvi. 19, he says the power of the keys was conferred on the Church "scilicet ut quisquis in Ecclesia ejus dimitti sibi peccata non crederet non ei dimitterentur; quisquis autem crederet, seque ab his correctus averteret, in ejusdem Ecclesiæ gremio constitutus, eadem fide atque correctione sanaretur."—S. August. de Doctrina Christiana Lib. i. c. 18.

"Ergo Petrus figuram gestabat Ecclesiæ; Ecclesia corpus est Christi. Recipiat igitur jam mundatas gentes quibus peccata donata sunt."—Ejusd. Serm. cxlix. c. 6. Cf. Enarratio in Ps. ci. Serm. ii. § 3.—Serm. ccxcv. c. 2.—Serm. cccli. c. 5.—De Agone Christiano c. 31.—Enchirid. c. 65.—Serm. cccxii. c. 3. It will be seen how nearly Luther followed in the footsteps of his master.

[3] Medicus bonus [Christus] ægros non solum præsentes sanabat sed et futuros etiam prævidebat. Futuri erant homines qui dicerent: Ego peccata dimitto, ego justifico, ego sanctifico, ego sano quemcunque baptizo. . . . Audet sibi homo hoc usurpare? Quid contra hæreticus? Ego dimitto, ego mundo, ego sanctifico. Respondeat illi non ego sed Christus: "O homo quando ego a Judæis putatus sum homo, dimissionem peccatorum fidei dedi." Non ego, respondet tibi Christus: "O hæretice tu cum sis homo dicis: Veni mulier, ego te sanam facio. Ego cum putarer homo dixi: Vade mulier, fides tua salvam te fecit."—S. August. Serm. xcix. c. 8.

We shall see hereafter that the heresy of the Donatists became the orthodoxy of Trent.

sharing it, and retains them in those who do not share it.[1] Yet with all his learning and acuteness St. Augustin had the vaguest possible conception of what was the nature of this mysterious power to bind and to loose. In one place he explains it by the judgments rendered by the martyrs who are to sit on thrones during the Millennium (Rev. xx. 4).[2] Again, in praying for the conversion of the Manichæans, he assumes that conversion and repentance will win remission of their sins and blasphemies, and if he refers casually to the power of the keys lodged in the Church, it is apparently only to indicate that by baptism in the Church they will be in a position to obtain pardon.[3] And yet again he argues that through the keys the Church has the power of inflicting punishment worse than death by the sword, by fire or by the beasts,[4] though the individual priest has no power; God pardons or condemns wholly irrespective of what the priest may say or do.[5]

For the next few centuries the question remained in the same state of fluctuation and uncertainty. On the one hand Cœlestin I. in 431 assumes the necessity of priestly ministrations by denouncing as murderers of souls those who refused penance to the dying.[6] Leo I., who was so strenuous a sacerdotalist, only ascribes to the priest as we have seen (p. 33) a deprecatory and mediatory power, but the exercise of this is essential to the reconciliation of the sinner. Zacchæus, in controverting the Novatians, claims the transmission of the grant from Peter, but limits it to sins that have been duly expiated, for the sentence of the bishop requires the assent of heaven.[7]

---

[1] S. Augustin. in Joannis Evang. Tract. cxxi. n. 4.

[2] De Civitate Dei Lib. xx. c. ix. § 2.

[3] De Natura Boni c. 48.

[4] Contra Adversarium Legis § 36.

[5] Quid volunt ut ego promittam quod ille non promittit? Ecce dat tibi securitatem procurator; quid tibi prodest si paterfamilias non acceptet? . . . Securitatem tibi procurator dedit: nihil valet securitas procuratoris. . . . Domini enim securitas valet etiamsi nolim; mea vero nihil valet si ille noluerit.—S. August. Serm. xl. cap. 5.

[6] Cœlestin. PP. I. Epist. iv. c. 2.

[7] Zacchæi Consultationum Lib. ii. c. 17-18.

H. C. Lea's extensive works : "A History of the
Inquisition of the Middle Ages," and "A Historical
Sketch of Sacerdotal Celibacy in the Christian Church,"
are written according to the very same methods as his
"History of Auricular Confession."